Christ and Caesar in Christian Missions

Christ and Caesar in Christian Missions

Edwin L. Frizen, Jr.
and
Wade T. Coggins,
editors

William Carey Library

1705 N. SIERRA BONITA AVE. • PASADENA, CALIFORNIA 91104

Library of Congress Cataloging in Publication Data
Main entry under title:

Christ and Caesar in Christian missions.

    Addresses and dicussions of the AEPM/EFMA/IFMA study
conference held in Overland Park, Kan., Sept. 25-29, 1978.
    1. Missions--Congresses. 2. Church and state
--Congresses. I. Frizen, E. L. II. Coggins, Wade T.
III. Association of Evangelical Professors of Missions.
IV. Evangelical Foreign Missions Association. V. Inter-
denominational Foreign Mission Association.
BV2390.C46   266   79-17124
ISBN 0-87808-169-0

Published by the William Carey Library
1705 N. Sierra Bonita Avenue
Pasadena, California 91104
Telephone (213) 798-0819

In accord with some of the most recent thinking of the academic press, the William Carey Library is pleased to present
this scholarly book which has been prepared from an author-
prepared and author-edited camera ready copy.

PRINTED IN THE UNITED STATES OF AMERICA

Contents

Preface

It is estimated that one-third of the world's population
lives under leftist totalitarian regimes. Millions of
others are under rightist governments or some limited form
of democracy. *The U. S. News and World Report* (December 4,
1978) reported that 64 nations are not free; 48 are partially free; and only 43 are free.

Christ and Caesar in Christian Missions came out of the
AEPM/EFMA/IFMA Study Conference held in Overland Park,
Kansas, September 25-29, 1978. This conference was spon-
sored by the Association of Evangelical Professors of
Missions, the Evangelical Foreign Missions Association, and
the Interdenominational Foreign Mission Association. The
purpose was to study crucial issues facing Christian missions in relation to diverse political systems. It was designed to enable executives and educators to provide guidelines for missionaries in understanding the influence of
their own political system on their theology and practice,
and to prepare them to cope with systems different from
their own. It was to call attention to curricular needs
in preparing new missionaries.

This volume contains four addresses by Dr. Earle Cairns,
which give the historical perspective and biblical basis
for response. The electives, small-group findings, and
discussions deal with practical concerns, specific issues,
and practical approaches.

   It is hoped that this book will provide help for missionaries under totalitarian regimes, and that it will assist
them in preparing the church for life in a hostile society.

                              Edwin L. Frizen, Jr.

May, 1978

PART I

Under Three Flags

Biblical Foundation

Earle E. Cairns

Mission, the perennial task of the church to make Christ known as the only Savior from sin, both in the Christian's homeland and abroad; and missions, the particular task of proclaiming Him as Savior in other lands (Matthew 28:18-20; Acts 1:8), takes place today in a changing and, more often than not, violent social order. This can be seen in many ways.

Through advanced means of travel, such as the jet plane and communication by short wave and satellites, the world has become technologically unified to the point where an ecumenical culture, strongly influenced by Atlantic civilization, is developing all over the world. At the same time, it is becoming economically and politically fragmented in spite of numerous economic and political agencies which are international in scope, such as the General Agreement on Trade and Tariffs and the United Nations. Secularism and materialism in various forms, one of the results of advanced technology, have more often been exported to other nations by the West than the spiritual values of civilization which made such advances possible. Arnold Toynbee spoke of this as the "apostasy of the West."

There has also been an unparalleled trek to the urban centers by masses from the rural countryside. Megalopolises with populations over ten million have appeared. Missions which have more often sought to reach rural areas will have to devise ways of reaching the unevangelized masses in the great cities.

Since 1914 European powers have been increasingly
eclipsed by the United States and Russia, and now the Arab
oil countries, in world leadership and influence. World
War I destroyed the Russian, Turkish, German and Austrian
Empires. The Great Depression of 1929 helped to weaken
their economies, and World War II brought about the disso-
lution of their empires in Africa and Asia. European nationalism was adopted by peoples of other lands in their
anti-colonial struggles and often had an anti-white bias.
The resurgence of older religions, such as Buddhism, Hindu-
ism and Islam, has provided the religious aspect of their
new nationalism.

These changes have stimulated a massive wave of revolutions in the twentieth century, especially since World War
II. Unlike the English, French, and American revolutions
of the seventeenth and eighteenth centuries which looked to
past Edenic models and sought the emancipation of the individual, modern revolutions have looked forward to Utopias
to be created by the revolutionaries after they had taken
over power. These revolutions often have been aggressive,
sought international power, and subordinated the individual
to the state as a means to state power. This has been the
case with the Nazi and Fascist revolutions of the right and
the Communist revolutions of the left. They have usually
had a secular religion of race, empire, or class which had
no room for the gospel of Christ and missionaries. Leftist
states have banned religion in favor of atheism and rightist
dictatorships, such as in Germany, wanting a paganized
Christian religion.

The missionary in such a world has a threefold responsibility, or operates under three flags. He is first of all a
member of an international brotherhood, the church of Jesus
Christ, the invisible organism of which he is an important
part. That church, entered only by the new birth (John
3:3, 5), has Jesus Christ as its supreme Head. The missionary is a part of the "colony of heaven" (Phil. 3:20, Moffat)
and has an overriding allegiance to Christ. This allegiance
is represented by the *Bible*. His *passport* represents his
allegiance to his homeland, the sending country to which he
has civic obligations. The *visa* on his passport, granted
by the government to whose land he is going as a missionary,
represents a third responsibility. He is a guest in that
land to serve Christ by evangelizing and serving its people.

His task is universal because the problems of the power

of Satan as the prince of this world, original hereditary
sin stemming from the failure of Adam and Eve in the garden
of Eden and unregenerate human nature, designated in the
Bible as the flesh, are present wherever man is found (Rom.
5:12, 19; Eph. 2:2-3; I John 2:15-17). This rift is tran-
scendental as well as earthly, and even affects nature (Rom.
8:16-17, 22).

This basic problem creates a need which can only be met
by the supernatural power of the gospel. Social service
will only treat the symptoms of the basic disease. It re-
flects the unbiblical optimism of the Greek, the Renais-
sance, and the Enlightenment concerning man and his nature
which they held was perfectible because man was not born
sinful, according to them. Thus, humanization, development or social action, to give the modern terminology, can
only be secondary and an outcome of preaching the gospel,
rather than the primary task of the missionary. Evangelization in fulfillment of the Great Commission of Christ is
his primary responsibility and has the highest priority.

Because the political environment of the missionary is
the modern nation-state, he must have a biblical view of
the state, understand the historical development of the
state, and seek to formulate principles for relationships
with the state in the light of the Bible and history.
These principles he can apply to his problems in his relations with states, and make applications which will expe-
dite the spread of the gospel.

THE BIBLICAL CONCEPTION OF THE STATE

Biblical Data and the State

The Bible has much more to say about the origins of the
state, and the limits of its power, and the responsibility
of the Christian to it than most people realize. Both the
Old and New Testaments provide material for a biblical foundation concerning the state and its legitimacy.

The Old Testament. The first mention that could relate
to the state occurs in Genesis 9:5-6. The text leaves one
with the clear impression that one shedding human blood for-
feits one's life, and will be punished by society organized
into a political order. Peaceful relations among men is a
primary responsibility of the state in order to uphold the
sanctity of human life.

Theocracy was the earliest expression of Hebrew political order after the patriarchal system was replaced by
judges. Religion was linked with political organization by
the priest-ruler who led both in religious and political
functions. Moses, Joshua, the era of the judges, and Eli
and Samuel, all in their turn had both political and religious leadership. This created a union of religion and the
state which has been the general pattern in those relationships until modern times in the United States.

These functions were separated when the children of Israel demanded a king in order to be like the surrounding nations. Both Moses and Samuel warned them of what would happen if they had kings, using words which very graphically
describe some of the problems of citizens concerning taxation and regulation in the modern state (Deuteronomy
17:14-20). Samuel several times uses the word "take" in
describing what would happen (I Samuel 8:6-22). Saul very
quickly violated this separation by arrogating the function
of priest to himself by offering sacrifice in the absence
of Samuel (I Samuel 13:8-13).

Even during the Babylonian captivity, men such as Daniel
and Jeremiah, continued to honor the state by serving pagan
kings loyally in civic matters, although holding finally to
spiritual allegiance as priority, if the king ordered them
to act against their conscience and religion. Jeremiah
urged that the captives pray for the state in which they
found themselves even though its leadership was pagan
(Jeremiah 29:7). Daniel and his associates loyally served
the Babylonian ruler until he demanded for himself worship
which belonged to God alone (Daniel 3, 6). Isaiah declared
that Cyrus was God's anointed (Isaiah 44:28; 45:1). David
would not take Saul's life when he found him sleeping because to him Saul was God's anointed head of the state (I
Samuel 24:6, 10). Jeremiah several times spoke of
Nebuchadnezzar, the pagan king of Babylon, as "my (God's)
servant" (Jeremiah 25:9; 27:6).

The writer of Proverbs counsels the godly man to recognize his dual obligation to God and to the king (Proverbs
24:21), and counsels against violent social change, both
in that passage and in Proverbs 17:11. The writer of
Ecclesiastes urges submission to royal power, particularly
when it is in tune with the divine will (Ecclesiastes 8:2,
4). Thus, the Old Testament writers believe that both
religion and the state come from God, and that each has its
proper sphere of authority over the individual whether the
ruler be good or bad.

The New Testament. A similar conception of the relation
of religion and the state is even more explicit in the New
Testament. John the Baptist did not condemn the service
tax officials and soldiers were rendering to the state, but
urged justice and order to be their criteria rather than un-
fair exactions and violence by the shedding of blood (Luke
3:12-14).

Christ clearly set forth the existence of two realms,
the civil and the religious, in His classic answer to the
Pharisees that they should give to Caesar what he could
rightfully claim and to God what was His rightful due of
worship (Matthew 22:21). He did, however, assert the overriding allegiance to God as the final spiritual power, if
civil authorities should ask for what belonged to God alone.
Civil authority came from God (John 19:11), but was sub-
ordinate to divine authority (John 18:36; Matthew 26:51-53).
Christ respected and accepted the proper claims of the
state by His willingness to pay taxes (Matthew 17:23-27)
and to leave matters of law to the judges (Luke 12:13-14).
During the temptation He did not dispute Satan's claim to
be the temporal sovereign of the kingdoms of the world.
Both the state and religion were granted to men by God.

The apostle Paul in passage after passage declared that
the state, along with the family and church, were institutions given by God for men's good. The power or authority
of rulers expressed in the word *exousia* was a part of that
divine authority which God had delegated to rulers in the
state to avoid anarchy. The same word is used by Paul in
Ephesians to express celestial authority, both good and
evil (Ephesians 1:21; 3:10; 6:12), as well as in Romans
13:1-7 for authority by human rulers in the state. In
Titus 3:1-2, as well as in Romans 13:1, he counsels obedience to magistrates because the power of the state is a
delegated part of the divine power, and resistance to such
power is resistance to the direct ordinance of God. This
power properly exercised punishes evildoers and rewards the
good. We must clearly keep in mind that Paul is not talk-
ing here about a particular form of government, but the fact
of government as an alternative to anarchy. There is no
divinely ordained form of government, but government as an
institution is ordained of God for human good.

Paul did not hesitate to make use of governmental sovereignty to protect his rights as a Roman citizen. At
Philippi he made the magistrates who had unfairly jailed
him come and release him (Acts 16:37-39). In Jerusalem he

used his citizenship to avert a severe beating (Acts 22:25-29). When it became essential to protect his life, he did not hesitate to appeal for trial before Caesar in Rome (Acts 25:7-12, especially verses 10-11).

Peter also recognized the proper human authority of the state, along with the divine authority, by his exhortation to obey the emperor (I Peter 1:13-17). One was to submit to every ordinance (*Ktisei*, creation) of man and to governors "for the Lord's sake" and because it was the will of God.

John claims that at the end of the present age, when the Antichrist arrogates supreme power to himself in religion and the state, that Christ at His coming will take back the authority that has been delegated to man in time and rule as a benevolent despot (Rev. 11:15). These views of the state by biblical writers were not blindly optimistic because they realized that the state could become demonic and take the place of God. Herod took to himself worship which belonged to God alone and suffered divine punishment (Acts 12:20-24).

Implications of the Biblical Data for Missions

Creation of the state. Paul believed that the coercive power of the state was not necessary for the righteous because they were under the coercion of an internal moral law which would cause them to do right even in the absence of an external law with sanctions (I Timothy 1:9), but was necessary to restrain evil and prosper goodness. The state was divine in origin so far as the fact of government was concerned, provisionally designed for man in time like marriage, and coercive in that it had delegated sovereignty from God to punish evildoers and to approve those who did good (Ecclesiastes 8:2; Proverbs 8:15; Daniel 2:21; 4:17, 25, 32). The state had its origin in the will of God to restrain evil.

While the Bible unequivocally asserts the fact that government is divinely ordained to seek peace abroad, to promote law and order domestically, and to permit its citizens freedom of conscience in their moral and religious life, it does not approve any particular form of government, such as monarchy, aristocratic oligarchy or democracy. It recognizes that men of low rank in society and even low moral standards may get control (Daniel 4:17; Acts 12:20-24) and pervert government by claiming power and even allegiance that belongs to God alone. It does not assert the superiority of one form over another. Paul and Peter both lived

and finally died in the reign of Nero who was one of the
most tyrannous and sinful of the Roman *princeps* in the first
century. Thomas Paine in *Common Sense* (p.1) made the re-
mark that "government, like dress, is the badge of our lost
innocence."

Although the Bible does not approve one form above another, and Christianity has been able to outlast even the
most tyrannous forms of government, democracy in some form,
while not essential to Christianity's well-being, seems to
have been the most compatible with the spread of Christianity. This may be because democracy implicitly recognized
the need for limitation of human power because of human sin
which will ultimately wreck any form of government unless
it is restrained by the sanction of the law. It is no acci-
dent that Latourette calls the nineteenth century "The Great
Century" for missions because the money and manpower of England in that period were dedicated to missionary activity
around the world. This was the period in which England
widened the representation in her democracy by giving the
middle and working class the vote. It was also the period
of major religious revival.

Claims of the state. If the state is of divine origin
for time, what claims can it rightfully make upon the individual and his property? It seems to be the clear teaching
of Scripture that *submission* to the rightful claims of the
state is enjoined upon the Christian. The various forms of
violent social change, such as rebellion and revolution,
are condemned (Proverb 17:11; 24:21). Man's recourse
against state claims that threaten his prior allegiance to
the claims of God is non-violent passive resistance or civil
disobedience. The apostles only refused to obey governmental authority when it demanded that they cease to preach
the gospel (Acts 4:19; 5:29). Otherwise, they were even to
suffer wrongdoing without protest, knowing that eternity
was more important than time, and the soul than the physical
body (I Peter 2:19). Joseph in Egypt and Daniel in Babylon
served the rulers faithfully until morality or their worship
of God were endangered. Rather than commit immorality or
fail to pray, both Joseph and Daniel went to prison and to
the lion's den. Thus, submission to the state is limited
to claims that are in the will of God for the state.

Support of the state by the payment of legally-levied
taxes and other dues is clearly set forth in Christ's teaching (Matthew 22:21; 17:24-27; Luke 2:1). Paul urged the
payment of taxes upon Christians (Romans 13:6-7).

The duty of *supplication* or prayer for government, even though we may not like its form or some of its actions, is a Christian responsibility. Jeremiah urged the Jews to seek the welfare of Babylon and to pray for its peace (Jeremiah 29:7). Paul specifically enjoins Christians to pray for kings and all that are in authority so that there may be peace abroad and domestic tranquility to facilitate the living of a Christian life (I Timothy 2:1-2).

Service to the state in terms of respect or honor was urged upon Christians both by Peter and Paul (Romans 13:7; I Peter 2:17). Those in power may at times not be worthy of honor or respect, but this does not excuse the Christian from proper recognition of authority.

Christian Compulsion. What should motivate the Christian as he views his obligations to the state? Peter and Paul suggest several motives that the serious Christian should consider as part of his Christian responsibility to the state.

Fear of punishment is suggested as one reason for submission and obedience. The violator of the law should expect punishment for his wrongdoing, even if he happens to be a Christian (Romans 13:4-5; I Peter 2:14). Conversely, a ruler--who recognizes his authority from God by delegation-- will reward conduct which is righteous. Paul also feels that our clear *conscience*, because we do that which is right to the state, is an important element of Christian conduct (Romans 13:5). Peter asserts that a desire to do the will of God in this respect is another motive to obedience. This will also avoid bringing *discredit* upon the name of God which Christians profess, and which pagans will ridicule if Christians do not fulfill their citizenship (I Peter 2:15). If these motives were important under the tyrannical rule of Nero, how much more important are they to the Christian today in a democracy in which he has a part through his vote, letters to his representatives, and the possibilities of public service in government if God calls him to that duty.

The Christian view of government is illustrated by Figure 1. Authority in the state comes from God by delegation to the people who in turn delegate authority to those who govern. Both the governed and the governors have clear lines of responsibility to God, and the governors and people alike have mutual responsibilities to each other. This view is one which is only partially realized in a

sinful world, but can be one which a Christian strives to
realize along with other Christians in the state. No form
of government is divine even though the authority of the
state is divinely willed and given. With Thomas Wentworth,
who went to the block in the reign of Charles I for his loyalty to that monarch who at the last disavowed him, we say
that we must not put our trust in princes who after all are
also but men (Psalm 146:3-5). The state is God's provision
in time to avoid anarchy until Christ sets up His theocratic state at His coming and brings all human authority
under His direct control (Daniel 7:14; Revelation 11:15).
In the interim, the Christian should support full religious
liberty and freedom of conscience in religious matters in a
state where there is a friendly separation of church and
state to assure maximum opportunity for the spread of the
gospel. The church alone is a part of eternity; the state
is but temporal.

FIGURE 1

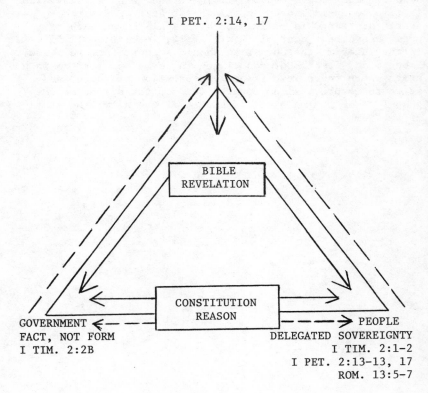

ABSOLUTE SOVEREIGN GOD

DAN. 2:21; ROM. 13:1-4, 6B

I PET. 2:14, 17

BIBLE
REVELATION

CONSTITUTION
REASON

GOVERNMENT
FACT, NOT FORM
I TIM. 2:2B

PEOPLE
DELEGATED SOVEREIGNTY
I TIM. 2:1-2
I PET. 2:13-13, 17
ROM. 13:5-7

KEY:
Authority   ————
Responsibility   — — —

Historical Development

Earle E. Cairns

The biblical relationship of church and state has been
variously interpreted through the centuries. Thus, it is
instructive to consider the course of religious history, to
be aware of these changes, and to see how they might be
helpful in the formulation of the Christian relationship of
religion and the state that may be useful to the missionary.
We are reminded by Paul in I Corinthians 10:6, 11 that history has a negative function in teaching us by example what
things to avoid. The apostle claims that the past has been
recorded "for our admonition." Paul also feels that the
past has a positive function--"for our learning" (Romans
15:4). The children of Israel were told that their children would want to know the meaning of the Passover (Exodus
12:26), and of the altar of stones commemorating the cross-
ing of the Jordan on dry land (Joshua 4:6, 21).

Relations between religion and the state have usually
fallen into two patterns. The state and religion have been
united in various combinations. Islam in Turkey, until
World War I, was above and guided the state in which the
Sultan had both civic and religious functions. The papacy
in the medieval Roman Catholic Church dominated the states
of Europe. In other unions religion has been dominated by
the state. The emperor in the Eastern or Orthodox Church
was more powerful than the patriarch in church affairs.
This caesaropapistic approach led to the secularization of
the church. The state churches of Germany, Scandinavia,
and England represent another type of union in which, except England, church leaders are paid by taxes raised by

the state, appointed by the state, and set forth no change
of doctrine or policy unless approved by the state.

The alternative to these various forms of union of religion and the state is a friendly or benevolent separation
of religion and the state. This was the case in the Roman
Empire from the Edict of Milan in 313 until 381 when
Theodosius finally linked the church and the state. The
earliest modern practice of this form occurred in the colonies of Rhode Island, Pennsylvania, and, to a more limited
extent, in Maryland during the seventeenth century. Separation seems more preferable to a union of the two.

THE EARLY CHURCH TO A.D. 313

Religion and the state were intimately united in the
Roman Empire. The emperor was *pontifex maximus* or chief
priest of the state religion, as well as leader of the
state. Christians were a minority under a hostile, increasingly authoritarian government as time went on.
Tertullian in his writings suggested that Christians refused to serve in the army and the civil service because of
their dislike of killing and because of the sacrifices to
pagan deities that accompanied military and civil service.
Up until 64, Christians had little trouble from the state
because they were identified as a sect of the Jews which as
a *religio licita*, or legal religion, was freed from such
civic duties.

Between 64 and 117, Christians became the victims of
local and sporadic persecutions by mobs or capricious magistrates. Domitian imprisoned John, and earlier Peter and
Paul suffered martyrdom under Nero. Ignatius died as a
martyr in the reign of Trajan.

From 117 to 250 following a ruling by Trajan in his letter to Pliny, governor of Bithynia, Christians fell under
the official ban of the state unless they would sacrifice
at state altars. Trajan ordered, however, that no action
was to be taken against them unless someone informed
against them. If they would not sacrifice, then their lives
were forfeited.

Between 250 and 313 persecution became universal and
violent because of imperial edicts. Decius in 250 ordered
all Christians to offer sacrifices. Those who did so were
given certificates to this effect. Those who did not, such
as Cyprian under Valerian, were executed on the spot.

Diocletian, faced with internal problems and external bar-
barian foes on the borders, ordered Christians to give up
Scriptures, destroyed their churches, imprisoned their
leaders, and continued the order that all should sacrifice
on pagan state altars. So many Christians were in prison
that Eusebius stated that there was not enough room for
criminals. This most severe persecution ended when
Diocletian retired to his splendid palace in Yugoslavia to
grow prize cabbages. Whether to receive those back into
the church who had given up Bibles became the occasion for
the severe Donatist schism in North Africa that rent that
church apart.

FREEDOM OF RELIGION 313-380

When Constantine defeated his rivals for the throne,
through what he felt was a sign from God of a cross in the
heavens with the motto "In this sign conquer," he issued an
order, the Edict of Milan, in 313. This edict gave full
freedom for all religions but did not, as so many mistakenly
think, make Christianity a state religion. He later favored
the church by exempting the clergy from military and civic
duties, by the grant of subsidies to rebuild churches, and
by making Sunday the official day of worship. In 314 at
Arles and in 325 at Nicaea, he used the force of imperial
power to get the church to deal with doctrinal divisions
which threatened the unity of the Roman Empire. It was
Theodosius, not Constantine, who made Christianity the
state faith in 380, by stating that the Catholic faith was
the only one to exist in the state, and in 381 making it
the state church and proscribing pagan religions. One
should speak of a Theodosian, rather than a Constantinian,
state church.

THE MEDIEVAL CHURCH   381-1517

In the West

During this era, there was considerable confusion as to
the relation of church and state, but in theory the Holy
Roman Empire of Otto after 962 exercised temporal power,
and the Holy Roman Catholic Church exercised spiritual
power. Universal church and universal state were the two
swords, or arms, of God. In practice, the Empire consisted
of over 300 small feudal states ruled by either high cler-
ics or feudal lords. One can say, though, that in the tendency to union, the church dominated the state through the
leadership of its able popes.

The church in the western part of Europe was a medieval,
bureaucratic, hierarchial institution which, through the
sacraments dispensed only by the hierarchy, had a corporate
monopoly on salvation. Outside the church there was no
salvation, according to such popes as Boniface VIII. The
pope had a triple tiara as the spiritual head of the
church, the ruler of a temporal state in Italy after 756,
and the claim to anoint and enthrone kings and emperors who
owed allegiance to him.

The growth of papal power had been gradual and illus-
trates the problem of historical accretions being added to
biblical truth. Bishop, or elder, and deacon were the two
major orders of church leaders in the New Testament, but in
the letters of Ignatius three orders of bishop, elder, and
deacon appear shortly after 100, with all bishops *equal* to
each other in honor and power. Cyprian and Jerome later
suggest that, while all bishops have equal power, the
bishop of Rome should have the first place of honor or
primacy to symbolize the unity of the church. By 445,
Leo I persuaded the emperor Valentinian III to recognize
the *supremacy* of the Roman bishop over all other bishops.
For all practical purposes, this marks the beginning of the
Roman Catholic Church.

Relations with the states of western Europe were important in the development of the supremacy of the papacy.
Leo I in 445 gained recognition from the temporal ruler
Valentinian III of the supreme power of the pope in the
church in all parts of the empire. Pope Gelasius I in 494
wrote to the emperor that there were only the powers of the
pope and the emperor in the world, but because at the judgment the pope must give account to God for the souls of the
rulers, rulers should submit to the authority of the papacy
in all matters. Pepin III, the Frankish ruler of what is
now France, in 754 promised the pope land in Italy and in
756 gave him a belt of land in central Italy. This marks
the beginning of the temporal power of the pope as the head
of a state as well as of the church. These lands were
taken by Italy in 1870, but the pope still heads the
Vatican state of over 100 acres, and he sends and receives
ambassadors, as does any head of state. The forged Donation
of Constantine which appeared at this time rationalized the
grant to the pope. The later pseudo-Isidorian Decretals of
the mid-ninth century further asserted the supreme power of
the pope over both clerical and lay officials. Gregory VII,
pope after 1073, in his *Dictatus Papae* claimed supreme
power for the papacy because the Roman church was founded

by God and was universal. It had never, nor could it ever, err to all eternity.

Innocent III, between 1199 and 1216, humbled Philip of France and John of England, who were rulers of rising nation states. He also defeated Otto III, the emperor of the universal Holy Roman Empire. Boniface VIII, in his bull *Unam Sanctum* shortly after 1300, claimed that one could not be saved except in the church and that one must admit the supremacy of the pope. The powerful nation-states of France and England kept him from carrying it out in practice.

By 1200 the Roman Catholic Church was at the peak of its power, but for various reasons it declined until the Reformation. Counter Reformation against Protestantism and inner Catholic renewal gave it a new lease of power. It was this institutional corporate spiritual monopoly through the sacraments dispensed only by the hierarchy that, with the aid of Spain, Portugal, and France in the days of empire building, Roman Catholicism was carried to Latin America, the Philippines, Indo-China, India, and briefly to Japan and China. France made Quebec solidly Roman Catholic. This expansion was culturally Latin and religiously homogeneous and Roman Catholic.

In the East

While the Roman pope became supreme over church and state in western Europe, the case was different in the East at Constantinople. Constantine in 330, to protect his eastern boundary, moved the center of government to the new city of Constantinople. When the last Roman emperor disappeared in 476 in the West, the pope was left to exercise temporal, as well as spiritual, power. The patriarch in the East, selected by the emperor and under his close supervision, fell under control of the state so that in the East the church was dominated by the state in any union of the two. Even in the present, the Eastern or Orthodox Churches are organized nationally, each with its own patriarch.

THE PROTESTANT REFORMATION 1517-1648

Two other forms of church organization appeared, besides the universal Roman Catholic, during the Reformation. Magisterial or state churches appeared in Germany, Scandinavia, Switzerland, Holland, Scotland, and England. Free churches were developed by the Anabaptists.

State Churches of the Reformation

Luther, Calvin, and other reformers had a theoretical
separation between the church and state, but in practice
they had something like a union of church and state in
which the two were interdependent. Luther believed that
Christians need no state because they obey an internal
spiritual law that causes them to be just but that in a de-
praved world some form of state was necessary to restrain
evil. Church and state were to be separate. Practical
necessity made him modify this position. In his pamphlet,
Address to the German Nobility, he urged the temporal
princes to reform the church, which refused to reform itself. The disorders of the Peasants Revolt in 1524 threatened continuance of the Reformation. The need for an
authority to supervise the church later led him to put
power into the hands of the princes. This control of the
church by the state has persisted in Germany. He would not
concede any right to the Christian to revolt against
authority. If the ruler asked one to act contrary to the
will of God in the Scriptures, he might then passively resist the ruler.

Calvin and Zwingli, who lived in the democratic Swiss
cantons, had a somewhat different approach, but in the end
even they closely linked church and state. Calvin believed
that the state was given by God to restrain evil and to
promote religion. Some form of aristocratic government by
the few, chosen by the many, was the best. He ruled out
rebellion against rulers who were accountable to God for
their treatment of their subjects. Obedience to the state
could be withheld if the ruler asked one to violate the
clear will of God revealed in the Bible. Geneva, Crom-
wellian England, Holland, and the Puritan colonies in
America derived their ideas of the relation of the church
and state from Calvin.

Cranmer and Hooker in England, because of the authoritarian rule of the Tudors, closely united the church to the
state. The Church of England under Henry VIII was a
national Catholic Church headed by the king before it became a Protestant state church in the days of Edward VI and
Elizabeth. This was because the king desired a legitimate
male heir, which did not seem possible unless he could divorce Katherine and get a new wife. When the papacy refused the divorce, he, in effect, nationalized the church
in England. The Reformation in England had a wide influence, because during the period of imperial expansion,

English Anglicans carried their church to the Thirteen
Colonies, Canada, South Africa, Australia, New Zealand, and
India. This first overseas empire provided the wealth that
made possible the financial base for the great English
missionary movement of the nineteenth century.

The Anabaptists

The Anabaptist ancestors of the Amish, Mennonites, and
Baptist groups were far ahead of their times in opposing
either universal Roman Catholic or Protestant state
churches. They desired to set up churches of baptized
believers which were to be separated from the state. They
would obey the legitimate demands of the state as an ordinance of God, but they would not take oaths nor serve as
soldiers or officials. Church and state were to be
strictly separated. Roger Williams carried these ideas to
the New World and in Rhode Island separated church and
state, as William Penn did later in Pennsylvania.

SEPARATION OF CHURCH AND STATE 1648-1919

The United States

After the short period of religious freedom in the Roman
Empire between 313 and 380, freedom of religion did not re-
appear until the early era of the Thirteen Colonies. The
Calverts, proprietors of Maryland, in order to get settlers
and provide an asylum of refuge for their persecuted Roman
Catholic compatriots, in 1634 set up that colony with freedom of religion for all except Unitarians and Jews. In
1636 Roger Williams in Rhode Island worked out complete
freedom of religion. Later in 1682 William Penn decreed
full freedom of religion in Pennsylvania, which soon became
a hodge-podge of religious sects. Both church and state
were to have freedom from each other under law. The church
was to be privately supported, and because of this, lay
leadership played an important part in the churches in these
states. The other nine of the Thirteen Colonies--three in
New England and six in the South--and New York opted for
established Congregational and Anglican churches. Thus,
the early colonists had experience in this land with state
churches.

During and after the American Revolution, the idea of
separation of church and state spread in the colonies. The
various states, such as Virginia in 1786, in their state
constitutions separated church from state and put support of

the church on a voluntary basis. The First Amendment to
the Constitution precluded any established or favored
church and banned any bar by Congress to the "free exercise
of religion." Article VI of the Constitution banned any
religious test or qualification for public office in the
new Republic. This led to the rise of national churches
supported by the laity; to a great extent because of this
support, the churches were governed by them. Numerous
cases later came before the Supreme Court that further defined the nature of the "wall of separation" between the
church and the state. Unfortunately, at times it seems as
if complete neutrality to religion and its divorce from
public affairs may lead to a secular state with leaders
bound by no religious principles. All churches do have
certain privileges, such as tax exemption for property used
for religious purposes, oaths on the Bible in court, the
name of God on coins, and the use of chaplains in the legis-
latures. This makes for a friendly separation and, ideally
at least, does not divorce religion from lawmakers' personal
lives.

France

   During the early days of the French Revolution, church
and state were separated, and church property was taken
over by the state. Napoleon in 1801, recognizing that the
majority of Frenchmen were Roman Catholics, negotiated a
concordat with the pope which became the basis of relations
between the church and state until 1901. In that year,
education was taken over from the church by the state and
secularized. In 1905, church and state were completely
separated, and state support of the clergy was ended. The
separation created a more secular state than was the case
in the United States with its friendly separation of the
two.

THE WARFARE-WELFARE STATE 1919-1979

   World Wars I and II led to increasing regulation,
rationing, and conscription of life and property to carry
on the wars, and accustomed people to government control
and reliance upon government. The Great Depression of 1929
led to demands for more control and services by government.
Disillusionment with democracy helped to create rightist
and leftist dictatorships in Italy, Germany, and Russia.
Calls for welfare services in democratic states led to increased taxation and government controls over life and
property. The new leftist, communist, totalitarian states

adopted an atheistic Marxian determinism which led them to separate the church from the state and to control the exercise of religion to the point where religion could be practiced but where only atheists could engage in public propaganda. Missionary work was banned in such lands because it was associated with capitalistic imperialism. Rightist totalitarian states have more often legally harassed missionary activity and have often set up a pagan counter-church, as was the case in Germany under Hitler. Missionaries will probably face increasing regulation in democratic countries, but it is still the most compatible form of government to give the church freedom to fulfill its mission. The church and missionaries should use all legitimate means to assure the fullest possible freedom of religion in order to carry out Christ's commission.

Principles of Action

Earle E. Cairns

What principles of action should govern the life and work of the missionary in the light of the biblical and historical data? Any missionary should have a sound biblical training which not only teaches him the contents of the Bible but how to study it for his own spiritual development. History will help to orient him in the present as he seeks to use the biblical and historical data to derive principles to govern his relation to the state.

SUBMISSION TO HUMAN GOVERNMENT

Submission or obedience to human government is clearly set forth in the Scriptures and enjoined upon the Christian, particularly he who labors under three flags. Scriptures such as Proverbs 24:21, Ecclesiastes 8:2, Daniel 4:17, Romans 13:1-7, and I Peter 2:12-14 emphasize loyalty to the ruler and to God as two important loyalties in the life of the Christian. One should notice that in these Scriptures the *fact* of Government as a divine institution is set forth, but no mention is made of approval for any particular *form* of government, such as democracy, aristocracy, or monarchy. The form is relative and changeable in time and space, but authority is eternal and absolute, coming from God and delegated to man. In fact, in Daniel 4:17 it is stated that God can set up the "basest of men" in authority. While this may refer to social rank, it may also suggest that sometimes in the permissive will of God and the failure of those governed, base men in a moral sense may get control of government. Certainly, the rise of numerous dictatorships

of the left and right since World War I illustrate how at
times base men may get control and can only be dislodged by
force.

The Scriptures leave no room for subversion or revolution against government. In Proverbs 24:21 and 17:11, the
righteous man is urged to have no part with rebellion or
men who want to bring social change by force. Obedience to
authority of the state is the alternative to chaos or anarchy or revolution. Peter was rebuked by Christ (Matthew
26:52-53) for trying to defend his Lord with the sword
against constituted authority when the Jews came to take
Christ captive. In periods of violence or revolution, the
Christian should avoid taking sides so that he might be a
mediator if possible. This will not stop him from doing all
he can to relieve suffering on both sides. It is at this
point that one might well take issue with the policy of the
World Council of Churches, which states that it cannot condemn those who resort to "violence as a last resort." When
David had the sleeping Saul (who was seeking David's life)
at his mercy, he refused to kill Saul because he was the
"Lord's anointed" to rule Israel (I Samuel 24:6, 12). Personnel can corrupt any form of government, and human history shows how quickly either the governor or the governed
may become corrupt. The effective democracies built for
the first time in human history in Athens and Rome did not
survive too long but soon came under some form of
dictatorship.

Even though the Scriptures do thus exhort obedience to
the authority of the state, there is limitation to that
authority. The principle of respectful protest--or even
passive or nonviolent resistance--can be adopted by the
Christian when the state goes beyond God-given boundaries
or violates the will of God as set forth in the Scriptures
concerning this relationship of man to the state. Christ
alone is Head of the Church, and the supreme allegiance of
the Church is to Him when the state is asking him to violate
that allegiance.

The state can even become demonic and anti-Christian in
its demands for worship by its subjects. Daniel's three
young Hebrew friends faced the terrors of the fiery furnace
rather than give to the king of Babylon the worship which
belonged to God alone (Daniel 3). When the Persian ruler
was persuaded to issue a decree that men could only pray to
Him for a limited period, Daniel, who had been a loyal and
trusted statesman, refused to cease his prayer to God even

in the face of the threat of the lion's den (Daniel 6).
Herod was punished directly and supernaturally when he allowed the people to give worship to him that belonged only
to God (Acts 12:21-23). The Confessing Church of Germany,
led by men like Barth and Niemoller, in 1934 set forth in
the Barmen Declaration the principles of government which
precluded the highest and final allegiance from being given
to anyone but God. Many, even at the cost of their lives,
have taken similar stands in the Communist left-wing
dictatorships.

   In addition to resistance to any state that claims the
worship which belongs alone to God, resistance also becomes
a proper course of Christian action when any government
bans the proclamation of the gospel. This may take the
form of legal petition or even, as in the case of Peter and
John, of disobedience. When they were forbidden to preach
the gospel among the Jews and were challenged because they
did so, Peter and John proclaimed their prior and higher
obedience to God; they went ahead and proclaimed Christ and
took the consequences of suffering that followed (Acts
4:10-20; 5:29). An extreme form of such consequences might
even be martyrdom, such as has been the fate of thousands
of Christians through the centuries. Archbishop Janani
Luwum of the Episcopal Church in Uganda is only the latest
and most notable martyr, allegedly at the hands of Idi Amin
in Uganda in 1977. The Scriptures even warn that suffering
might befall the church as it stands for the gospel
(Matthew 10:34; Acts 14:22; 15:26; I Peter 2:19; 4:12).

   Other religious persons who withstood the will of the
ruler when it violated the will of God at times adopted
flight as the proper answer. The early Christians re-
treated to Pella in A.D. 70 when the Romans besieged the
city. During the first persecution, Cyprian, for the good
of his church, yielded to urging that he flee and hide until
the end of the persecution so he could later help the
church. Subsequently he did, in another persecution, will-
ingly suffer martyrdom. The Huguenots in France were
forced to flee in 1685 when Louis XIV put their worship
under the ban. Nearly 200,000 of them went to England, the
Thirteen Colonies, Holland, and South Africa. Only
recently, Festo Kivengere had to flee from Uganda.

   Obedience to the authority of the state, except when it
demands worship that belongs to God alone or bans the witness to Christ by the Christian, seems to be clearly enunciated in the Bible. When suffering comes because of the

exceptions, the church should remember that the state is
temporal and not eternal and that it has power over the
body alone and cannot destroy the human spirit that is
solely dedicated to the will of God. It should be noted
that Herod was promptly punished physically (in time) when
he accepted worship which should have only been given to
God. It should also be kept in mind that the coming of
Christ is imminent and that human authority will give way
to His authority at His return (Revelation 11:15). A
Christian and biblical philosophy of history will help one
to keep these matters in proper perspective.

SEPARATION OF CHURCH AND STATE

The wisdom of a friendly or benevolent separation of
church and state is a logical implication from the principle of submission to the state and seems to be justified
by history. Such separation should never be construed to
mean that the leadership of the state should be irreligious
or without ethical principles. The "wall of separation" is
legal rather than moral and spiritual, for the state derives
its authority from God alone. Such separation precludes an
established church or any violation of the principle of a
free conscience in the phrase "free exercise thereof" (of
religion) in the First Amendment to the Constitution.
Americans were to have no established church nor interfer-
ence with freedom of conscience and worship. Any religious
test for public office was also banned in Article VI of the
Constitution.

American Christianity has responded well to this climate
of opinion. Nowhere in the world are larger sums voluntarily contributed for religious purposes or do more people
give freely and voluntarily of their time than in this land.

Recognition of religious influence in public life is
seen in the provision of chaplains in our legislative halls
and the armed services, the phrase "In God We Trust" on our
coins, and the name of God in the Oath of Allegiance.
Christians should continue to support the principle of
separation but insist that this does not necessarily mean
that the state and its leadership must be neutral--or even
hostile--to religious and ethical principles. Only one
committed to Christ and theologically informed has a sound
basis for an ethical system that will result in conduct
pleasing to God.

France also has a strict separation of the church and
the state, but religion is excluded from education or public

functions. The state is secular and unrelated to religion.
All religions are equal under the law. There has not been
the penetration of ethical and religious principles into
government nor into the lives of the governors that there
has been in the United States.

Totalitarian states of the left have, at least in the
initial stages of setting up government, separated the
church from the state but have then gone on either to ban
religion or severely limit worship. Rightist dictatorships
have sought to dominate religious life and to manipulate
the churches to blindly support the state. Hitler promoted
his own brand of church, which was semi-pagan.

The Christian and the missionary at home and abroad
should strive legitimately to separate church and state so
that what respectively belongs to Caesar and to Christ is
clearly delineated. This will help to create a climate of
opinion that will be most conducive to the spread of the
gospel at home and abroad.

LIMITED POLITICAL INVOLVEMENT

Because his primary allegiance as a "citizen of heaven"
is to Christ as the Head of the church, the missionary has
to think out what is a legitimate political involvement for
him as a citizen of his homeland and as a guest in the land
where he serves as a missionary.

His passport is a symbol of his responsibility to the
land from which he comes. When proximity or consular and
ambassadorial services make it possible, he has a responsibility to participate in the political life of his own
state as far as he can. Paul both urged participation in
service to government and made use of its facilities in the
promotion of the gospel. The missionary can keep himself
informed as far as possible on events in his own land and
vote with an absentee ballot to help choose parties, policies, and personnel to participate in the governing of our
land.

He may have to refuse government largesse or aid if that
would involve himself or his mission in activities that
would make his major work of proclamation of the gospel
difficult. This is especially the case if his work would
link him with the so-called imperialism of his own country
and make him unacceptable in the land where he has been
called to minister. Missions should carefully evaluate how

far their personnel should cooperate with their home government or have associations with military, consular or
embassy officials abroad. They might even unwittingly become linked with intelligence agencies in a way that might
have an adverse effect on their work at a later time.

While the missionary might have a deep affection for
American democratic institutions and free enterprise as the
best forms of economic and political organization for
society, he should remember that his work is spiritual and
dedicated to planting the church in other lands in fulfillment of Christ's commission. He must remember that our
systems of political and economic organization have a long
history of practice and theory in England and the Thirteen
Colonies and that these systems matured very slowly and
haltingly. Many lands to which he will go have only recently been exposed to democracy, and even where it is
adopted, these lands often backslide into some form of
totalitarianism. He will leave the task of urging these
principles upon our consular and embassy representative.

The question of the extent of his political involvement
also comes up in his relation to the government of the land
in which he is a guest to preach the gospel. This relationship, symbolized by his visa, may vary at different times
and under different circumstances. Certainly he will take
care--courteously and patiently--of the legal necessities
to establish proper legal residence in that country, even
though it may consume much time and cause some inner irri-
tation. He will also obey the legitimate laws of that land
as they apply to his work and life. He will be courteous
to, and friendly with, public officials, but not to the
point where he might be identified with a particular fac-
tion or party. He should be neutral concerning politics
but urge the national Christians to fulfill their legitimate duties as citizens. In the case of violence, he will
aid the suffering on all sides and try to serve as a
neutral mediator to end conflict when he can. In cases of
oppression, he may want to advise national Christians on
how to make their opinions known to the government. In
extreme cases, he might even have to withdraw for the good
of the national church. Such was the case in Vietnam. He
is not responsible to glorify, or even publicly approve,
government which may be adverse to human freedom or the
spread of the gospel.

AVOID CULTURAL OR ECCLESIASTICAL NATIONALISM

There is no place for feelings, or manifestation in word
or action, of cultural superiority nor for social separation
from national Christians on the part of a missionary.
Cultural superiority complexes may well result in so-called
"culture shock" because one is so wedded to one's own culture that one cannot adapt to the differences inherent in
another culture. This may become an increasing problem as
one resides longer in the guest country. One has to remember that the church is one body by the Spirit (I Corinthians 12:13), and in that body there is no room for feelings of superiority or physical separation. Scriptures
such as Genesis 1:26-27; Acts 10:34-35; 17:25-26; John 4:9;
Romans 5:12, 19; Ephesians 6:9; and Colossians 3:25 set
forth this physical and spiritual unity clearly. The missionary as a guest in another land will try to be flexible
and adaptable in matters of dress, customs, food and facial
color; and he will seek, as a servant of Christ, to avoid
superiority in word, deed, or manner. Unlike nineteenth
century missionaries who sought often both to convert and
civilize nationals, he will remember that his mission is
primarily spiritual. Knowledge of the history, language,
and culture of the people to whom he goes will be invalu-
able in helping to overcome feelings of social superiority
or to avoid culture shock. People everywhere will respond
to a genuine love and friendship which respects the differences that may exist in culture. Culture in itself is
not sinful, but elements in it that are sinful must, whether
in his homeland or where he serves, be brought under the
judgment of the Scriptures.

The missionary will avoid an ecclesiastical nationalism
that makes him feel that only the home forms of polity and
theology should be used in the organization of the local
national church. Instead, he will seek to help the national Christians find out from Scripture what is the best
form of polity in their situation.

He will not want to indulge a ghetto complex or live in
a missionary compound that separates him from the national
Christians. Too often, in resting from their work, missionaries may limit social intercourse to their own national group and leave the national Christian with the
feeling that he is a second-class citizen of the kingdom of
God. He need not even feel that he must defend the actions
of his home country, whether right or wrong, but admit its
weaknesses and point out how it has tried to serve others.

Travels in many countries where one could observe the
relations of the missionary and national Christians for a
period leave the author convinced that the most helpful
missionaries have identified themselves closely with the
national Christians and have led them in the Scriptures to
form churches which take into account legitimate facets of
their own culture which do not clash with biblical standards. He will let them be Christians in their own culture
under the   judgment of the Scriptures and the leadership of
the Holy Spirit. He will thus avoid forcing upon them his
"cultural baggage" or "overhang" from his homeland. They
may wish to develop their own music, liturgy, lay witness,
and forms of biblical instruction. Thus, he will avoid
idolizing and exporting his own national or ecclesiastical
institutions and culture.

Instead, like Paul, he will not neglect the increasing
number of large urban centers but will evolve a Christian
urban strategy for spreading the gospel to meet the needs
of those in the cities. He will seek to create self-
governing, self-supporting, and self-propagating churches
led by the Holy Spirit and under the judgment of the Word.
Mission society leaders and missionaries would do well to
again study the book of Acts in the development of scriptural principles in a day of growing authoritarian governments and nationalism.

THE PRIORITY OF PROCLAMATION

Siren voices today seek to lure the missionary into
revolution in the help of Christ to liberate people from
oppression in order to create a Marxist or democratic
socialist state. Several theologians have developed a
"theology of liberation or revolution." They overlook
Christ's statement that His kingdom was spiritual and
could not be spread by force (Matthew 26:52; John 18:36).
Missionaries will be sympathetic with the oppressed and
seek to relieve their sufferings and guide them to make
whatever legitimate protest that can be made in the limits
of their political system, but the work of missionaries is
the nonviolent proclamation of the gospel and not revolution or liberation.

Other voices call him to engage in development or humanization, the present code words for the liberal orientation
to missionary service. He will, as an outcome of the gospel, seek, in natural disasters or man-made crises, in war
or revolution, to relieve suffering and to aid refugees in

the emergency. He may even help in development by drilling
wells and by introducing new crops and animals for better
food, and hospitals to meet physical needs, but he must never
lose sight of his main goal: to represent Christ and to
win men to Him by the gospel. Development serves to meet
physical needs in time, but spiritual needs that fit man
for eternity must have the priority. The accompanying
chart shows the difference between those who support liberation or development and humanization and the missionary
whose main task is the proclamation of the gospel. He has
continuity of message with the early church, even though
his methods may differ from those of the past. The gospel
involved evangelism to save, baptize, and disciple; fellowship in the only true, international brotherhood, the
church; service as the conscience of the world by preaching,
which applies the gospel to society by enunciating the principles of social and personal ethics; and service to those
in need, beginning with those in the church first and then
reaching to others (Galatians 6:10). Richard Baxter re-
minds us in *The Christian Directory* (Part I, Ch. 3) that
"in doing good prefer the souls of men before the body."

PRAYER

It seems like "carrying coals to Newcastle" to urge
prayer upon missionaries as a principle, but the Scriptures
suggest the importance of prayer. Paul urged prayer for
all men, as well as those in authority in I Timothy 2:1-2.
Verse 4, as well as Romans 2:4 and II Peter 3:9, link
prayer with the will of God to have all men come to know
Christ. Too often missionary meetings, conferences, and
policy sessions are devoted to finding out programs and
policies that might be useful, rather than to prayer that
will reveal what seems "good to the Holy Ghost and to us"
(Acts 15:28).

Such prayer should be in the Holy Spirit (Romans 8:26-27).
Only then will there be the real prayer and a "burden" for
the cause of Christ. The writer has noticed in the study of
revival that earnest prayer was one of the most common pre-
cursors of major revival. This should have high priority in
the life of the missionary.

REVIVAL

Church history has been marked by periodic revivals in
crises when it seemed as if the church would go under its
burdens or be destroyed. These revivals, which were of

Christians, were marked by prayer and the study of the Bible under the judgment of the Holy Spirit. One cannot but wonder whether the high percentage of Koreans who are Christians is not due to the revival of 1907, in which nationals and missionaries studied the Bible, prayed, and made whatever confession was needed to each other or to the group, and then went out and witnessed to Christ.

PURITY OF LIFE

Example plays a large part in the development of Christian character (I Corinthians 11:1; Titus 2:7; and I Timothy 4:12). The character of Daniel and his friends (Daniel 1) won for them the opportunity to serve God as they felt best. Low standards of morality from pagan backgrounds or perverted Christianity may plague national churches. Here, by word and example of the highest personal ethical standards, the missionary can serve best.

These principles will help in God's program for God's people in our day. Thus will we serve our day as David did "his own generation" before "falling on sleep" (Acts 13:36).

TABLE 1

THE FUNCTION AND FUTURE OF THE CHURCH

Liberal

Social structures--sin in environment
Social action to civilize
Justice
Horizontal--love to man
Service for temporal, physical
    well-being

Saved in and by service
Kingdom on earth by man
Works
Society (corporate)
Post-Millennial
Church will cleanse world of racism, war,
    injustice and inequality

God is immanent
Transform society by education and
    legislation

Stress sociology and political science

This-worldly orientation
Direct social action by church
Man-centered
Social conscience
Final solutions in history often
    socialistic
Utopian order
Reforms or revolution

TABLE 2

THE FUNCTION AND FUTURE OF THE CHURCH

Evangelical

Sin in individual by heredity
Evangelism--proclamation of gospel
Justification
Vertical--relate to God by faith
Salvation of eternal soul

Saved to serve
Church, Christ's bride
Faith
Individual
A- or Pre-millennial
Cataclysmic supernatural end to age

God is transcendent
Transform individual by new birth

Stress theology

Other-worldly orientation
Indirect social action through individuals
Christ-centered
Spiritual conviction
Proximate solution to man's problems in
    time, final beyond history
Millennium (Eden regained)
Renovation

The truth is not in this "either/or" but in "both/and."
The task of the church is first evangelism (Matthew 28:18-
20; Acts 1:8) to relate persons vertically to God by faith.
These persons then will show love in action in society as
they occupy until their hope (Christ's second coming) becomes fact (Ephesians 2:10; I Corinthians 3:11-12; Titus
3:8).

Problems
and Applications

Earle E. Cairns

Constant, accelerating, irresistible, and pervasive
social change has been a characteristic of the modern world,
especially in the twentieth century. Such change has come
in technology so that through shortwave radio, TV, satellites, transportation by jet, and other means the world has
become a "neighborhood." Newer methods of fabrication of
goods in factories have produced more goods. Rising expec-
tations have been created in backward lands through radio
and TV. Ethical and religious absolutes, which uphold the
value of the individual and his ethical relation to his
fellows and religious relation to God, have been dropped in
favor of situation ethics and existential forms of human-
istic religion.

Social change may be defined as the legal or violent re-
construction of institutions and culture to correct real or
imagined social imbalances. There are several kinds of
social change. Some reject it and *retreat* from society as
did the Qumram community or medieval monks. Spain in the
Philippines *rejected, resisted,* and *repressed* attempts at
social change. The Czar of Russia in 1905, after a short
uprising, redressed grievances by granting a duma, which
was an elected assembly representative of the people to
advise the Czar. *Reform* to correct social grievances has
been successfully practiced by the British upper classes,
who granted representation to those lower in society in the
nineteenth century and in their empire gave self-government,
which eventuated in the British Commonwealth.

Social change may be promoted by violent means, such as a riot, the spontaneous action of a mob; insurrection, which is an organized, guided mob seeking social change; a *coup d'etat*, which changes only the personnel running the government; rebellion, which seeks to change institutions by force; civil war, a form of internal war; and most widely used, revolution, to overthrow the existing order.

Revolution has been a characteristic of modern history, and revolutions have been increasing in frequency, violence, and bloodshed since World War I. Table 3 (on pages 43-44) reveals the differences between more democratic revolutions, beginning with England in 1689, and totalitarian revolutions since World War I. The former revolutions resulted in increasing freedom for the individual, but the latter have led to oppression of the individual by the state, which is the only political entity of importance to these revolutionaries. Leftist communistic totalitarian states ban control of property for production to the individual, whereas rightist states permit him to hold it subject to the will of the government. Both ban any personal liberties, and both were set up by violent means. This creates the terrible problem of power without the discipline of "love" or a "sound mind" (II Timothy 1:7).

Christ never advocated violent social change, and He came to fulfill, rather than destroy, the past. He clearly taught and practiced obedience to rightful claims of government. Most revolutions, even the democratic Lockean revolutions, are based on a false view of man as good and perfectible. They have a false eschatology which suggests that Utopia can come by human governance: salvation is in history by man. They are based on terror and violence and are often anti-Christian and atheistic. They may begin in idealism but too often end in opportunistic corrupt control of power. Human lives--as in the tragic takeover in Cambodia, where it is estimated 1.2 million of a population of 7 million in 1975 have lost their lives by the end of 1977--are counted of little value compared to the existence of the state. Communism in various lands, Nazi and German Fascism, South American dictatorships, and some Arab states are examples of totalitarian dictatorship. Those of the right are usually less brutal than those of the left in terms of total loss of life in establishing the "New Order."

THE SECULAR STATE

The area of freedom in the face of revolutions such as
these has been shrinking. Freedom House of New York estimated that at the end of 1977 only 35% of the people in the
world in 44 nations and 25 territories were free; 47 had
partial freedom, and 64 were not free. Even in those that
were free, religion was facing increasing problems through
the increase of governmental regulation by the secular
state, supposedly neutral to religion. This has created a
problem for religion to the point where, in many states,
the church is coming to understand the feelings of the
Christians in the Roman Empire.

The Warfare-Welfare State

The warfare-welfare state has even brought limitations
on religious freedom and conscience in democratic states
through increasing regulation. Private Christian schools
have, in several states in the United States, been brought
to court by government to enforce state regulations concerning education. Private institutions under religious
leadership have also been brought to court for not meeting
state standards for corrective institutions, such as those
for wayward girls. Missionaries have increasing difficulties getting permission to enter India for missionary work,
and laws to ban conversion have been passed by some of the
Indian states. In the late summer of 1978, Indonesia
threatened missions by decrees of the minister of religion.
These decrees limited literature distribution or door-to-
door visitation and ordered foreign organizations to train
nationals so that in two years Indonesians could take over
positions held by foreigners. Israel's new law, which
mandates fines or prison for those giving "inducements" to
people to change their religion, will hamper missionary
work in that supposedly democratic land. Internal Revenue
Service regulations for religious bodies will involve extra
costs and eventually create problems of separation of church
and state for missionary endeavor.

Failure of governments to live within a balanced budget
and the running of large annual deficits in democratic
countries have been major factors in the virulent inflation
affecting the world. The value of the dollar in terms of
the Japanese yen has been nearly halved. This means a
doubling of the cost of living for missionaries in Japan,
in addition to the Japanese inflation. Mission executives
will be increasingly struggling with this problem.

Christian citizens, missionaries, and their organizations should take all legitimate means to ensure balanced
budgets in their lands and a minimum of regulation by
voting for men promoting fiscal soundness and a necessary
minimum of regulation. They can also contact their representatives through letters, phone, or other means. Offenses
in other states against freedom of conscience in religion
can be reported to our State Department for proper action.

Totalitarian States

Totalitarian states of the left, in the initial stages of
revolution, usually separate church and state on the grounds
of the linkage of the church with former repressive elements in government. Religion is banned; or if it is permitted to exist, it can only be practiced in licensed places
and cannot be proclaimed publicly. The aim is the final
elimination of religion so that atheism, the official religion of Communism, will triumph. Harassment of various
kinds is practiced against the church; and in many cases,
prison or martyrdom has resulted when Christians have tena-
ciously held to their faith. The days of Diocletian, with
severe persecution of the church, have been re-created in
many countries. Needless to say, missionaries will not be
granted admission to these lands, and Bibles in sufficient
numbers cannot be published.

Rightist totalitarian states have not usually banned religion but, as in the case of Nazi Germany, sought to
create a semi-pagan rival church and put strong Christian
leaders in concentration camps. Christians have been
harassed in seeking education and employment. Missionaries
have not been admitted. Usually, rightist totalitarian
states have not been so virulently anti-Christian as leftist Communist states, which are officially atheistic.

How can missionary organizations act in such lands to
help the national Christians carry on their Christian life,
witness, and worship? Where he is still permitted to work
in totalitarian countries, the missionary will keep in mind
that his main task is not social change but the proclamation
of the gospel in various ways. He will remember that the
kingdom of God is not dependent upon a particular political
or economic system and that the church has survived under
varying systems. Democracy, rather than dictatorship, is
the more modern and unusual form of political organization
in human history. He will bear in mind while in the new
third world lands that democracy at home evolved very

slowly. If he and the national Christians do not hew to
their spiritual priorities, the church can disappear as it
did in Carthaginian North Africa; in ancient China, where a
strong Nestorian Church was lost; in Japan in the seventeenth century, when Roman Catholicism was wiped out; and
in Albania in our day.

Missionaries need special preparation for work in lands
where freedom is limited. They should obtain a knowledge
of the history and nature of the systems under which they
will live and work. The writings of Marx and Lenin, good
biographies of these men, and helpful secondary histories
will enable them to make a distinction between totalitarian
Communism and various democratic socialistic states in
Africa and Asia. "Know your enemy" is a good rule. The
missionaries will, in contrast, seek to develop a Christian
philosophy of history; its concept is that God created the
universe through Christ and that man is to be one with his
fellows in trust. The dualism in history between sinful
men and systems and those seeking to do the will of God becomes clear with the doctrine of the fall. In the course
of history, Christ and the church have been the means of
salvation, informing the world of God's love in Christ.
The consummation of history is in the hands of the coming
Christ, rather than in the hands of men seeking to create
Utopia through the action of the secular state.

Personal discipleship should be an important part of the
missionary's education. He should come to know biblical and
theological content and should cultivate the ability to use
the Bible for his own personal development and to disciple
others. The practice of prayer will be an important part of
his preparation, to give him day-by-day stability and
steadiness in time of crisis. Study of anthropology of the
area in which he is to serve and of the liberal arts will
help him to be flexible and adaptable and to avoid "culture
shock" and "cultural overhang." Above all, attention to a
simple style of life is important to create a humble, serving attitude to the national church in the spirit of I Peter
5:1-3. The ideals of I Thessalonians 1:5 will become a
reality in his ministry.

The matter of missionary witness in lands closed to missionary activity, in totalitarian Communist or Muslim lands,
should be given careful consideration. Through radio Bible
reading, Bible truth is possible for those who do not have
access to Bibles. Radio Bible schools train lay leaders to
lead family, cell, or house churches in lands where public

worship and preaching of the gospel is limited. FEBC in
the Pacific and HCJB in Latin America have done an excel-
lent job in this way. The formation of house or cell
churches may be the only way for Christian fellowship. The
church may even have to "return to the catacombs." Engi-
neers, lay persons entering these lands at the invitation
of government to perform business functions, and many others
may find opportunities for personal witness and fellowship
with Christians who feel so isolated in such an environment.
Witness to nationals permitted to go abroad by their governments, if linked with Christian love, may win converts who
can go back home to form a nucleus for a Christian group.
Businessmen, diplomats, and students can be contacted.
Above all, the ministry of prayer for those in lands where
religious freedom is abridged will be helpful. Prayer can
strengthen Christians to stand and even bring about, in the
plan and will of God, changes in government. We can urge
our own Government, as President Carter has done, to stand
for human rights, including freedom of conscience and religion. Our Government can also bring violations to the
attention of the United Nations, which has too often been
selectively concerned with such violations on the part of
rightist dictatorships, while ignoring such violations by
the left.

NATIONALISM

Nationalism is closely related to the problem of the increasingly secular states, whether democratic or totalitarian. It is an emotional feeling of kinship of people in
an organized state which is based on real or imagined common interests.

It may be an ecclesiastical nationalism in which a particular religion is linked to the state. Several Muslim
states have banned missionaries and made converts face the
threat of death for becoming Christian. Buddhist states
like Burma have banned missionaries, but the Christian witness has been carried on by nationals. We will, like Paul,
have to entrust the local Christians to preach the gospel
by life and, where possible, by word in such situations.
We will pray for them and, if possible, develop paramission
ministries through hospitals, schools, and other means which
may be permitted.

Cultural nationalism in lands where missionaries can
work, as in Africa, may lead to the formation of separatist
(and in some cases, heretical) religious groups under a

national leader. Africa has, according to authoritative
studies, 6,000 such groups with about 7,000,000 people in
34 countries, including 290 tribal groups which exist along-
side the regular denominations and mission churches.

Anti-colonialism or imperialism is the other side of
cultural nationalism. Missions were forced on China, along
with opium, in 1858 after the second Opium War. Perhaps
this, along with the takeover of educational missions by
Liberals, account for the disappearance of institutional
Christianity in Communist China. The missionary can admit
the mistakes of past imperialism, but he can also point out
the rise of a new wave of Communist imperialism which is
even more repressive than any past imperialism of European
nations. He can remind nationals of the training of many
of their leaders in mission schools, the rise of their educational systems, written languages, hospitals, and new
crops. European imperialism, especially that of England,
has been self-liquidating through the grant of representative, then responsible government, and finally independence
or autonomy in the Commonwealth. After all, men like
Ghandhi learned their ideas of democracy in British institutions of higher education. Such reminders would have to
be given in a humble manner.

A missionary should watch his own cultural nationalism
so that it does not lead him to associate only with fellow
missionaries. Christian hospitality surely should include
Christian nationals. The Scriptures urge such hospitality
(Romans 12:12; Hebrews 13:2; III John 6, 8).

STATE PERSECUTION

Even though the land where he serves may be democratic
or a benevolent, paternal dictatorship, the missionary must
be awake to the possibility of rapid and violent social
change, and he must help the national church to prepare for
such a situation. Christian faith is no guarantee that
either the Christian or the church may not have to suffer
in a world in which nearly two-thirds of the people live
under authoritarian governments.

The missionary will work to train national leadership in
Bible memorization in case the Bible is later banned. He
will seek to make them aware of biblical content and techniques of Bible study, as well as having a sound system of
biblical doctrine to give stability. This training will
also include training in church organization and discipline.

He will, as fast as possible, commit the national church to
national leadership so that if he has to leave, the church
can continue. National leaders should be taught how to
form small cell or house churches. Multiple trained lay
leadership is essential so that if one is removed by imprisonment, another can take his place. John Wesley made
effective use of the class meeting, which is a cell-group
type of organization.

     If violent change does occur in the land in which he
serves, the missionary must have a clear idea of what
course of conduct he should follow under the guidance of
the Holy Spirit, the counsel of colleagues, and that of the
national leaders. He can identify with those who suffer
because of violence by medical aid and care for refugees.
He should try to avoid attachment to either side, so that
he can be a mediator who will be trusted by both sides. If
oppressive local agencies violate the law by force, he can
help the nationals plan a respectful, legitimate protest to
government. If he is forced out, he may, as a citizen, want
to give his government the facts and urge it to use the
moral force of the United Nations on behalf of the nationals. He may even face expulsion in matters of conscience that pit him against government or rebel edicts.
Even dictators want to be popular, but there is a limit to
power; once this limit is passed, counter-revolution may
result. In times of peace, the missionary can urge upon
the national church the exercise of biblical citizenship in
terms of voting, public service, and contact with those in
authority.

     In times of violence, it may be wise--after consultation
with colleagues and national leaders and prayer--to leave
an area of service. When his state department urges evacu-
ation, at least women and children should be moved out. If
the proclamation of the gospel is banned, and the missionary's presence becomes an embarrassment to the national
church, he will feel free to leave without any thought of
cowardice. He will try to help the national church to see
that suffering may be a part of the cost of following
Christ, as it was in the early church for Stephen, Peter,
and Paul. Martyrdom might even be a possibility to be
faced in the will of God. Certainly many Christians today
face such a possibility in different nations. Some suffering may be because of past sin, be educational, or be disciplinary (Job 3:10; Proverbs 3:11-12; Hebrews 12:6-10); be
for the glory of God (John 9:13; 14:4, 15); or be used to
train us to better help others at a later time (II Corinthians 1:5-6). He will be aware that before Christ gave

the great commission, He stated that all power was His. After stating the great commission, He said that His presence would be with His servants in all situations (Matthew 20:18, 20 cf. 19).

PERSONAL ETHICS IN GOSPEL WITNESS

Ethical problems have arisen in missions as missionary organizations and missionaries have faced several problems: getting Bibles to fellow-Christians in lands where they are banned; entering the country as a secular worker but intending to use that entry to have a chance to preach the gospel; telling the truth at borders when entering a land; or what to do when religious meetings are banned. If confronted with two situations where the truth does not seem absolutely clear, one may have to choose a gray in the absence of a clear white situation. One will give information if directly asked, but he need not volunteer more than is asked. Prayer may lead to the distraction of an official from a particularly difficult situation. The policy of honesty seems best in all such situations.

Whatever the problems, the lordship of Christ should be held high. He alone is the Head of His church. Methods of proclamation may change, but there must be a continuity of message with the early church. One under His call goes to minister as a servant, not a superior. He will remember that the Lord Who called him has all power (John 13:3; 17:15, 22) and has promised to be with him to the end of the age.

TABLE 3

SOCIAL, POLITICAL, AND ECONOMIC CHANGE BY REVOLUTION OR EVOLUTION

Totalitarianism	*Democracy*
By revolution, 20th century	By revolution or ballots, 17th-20th centuries
Utopian future	Restoration of Edenic past
Discontinuity	Continuity
Representative, 1 party	Representative, responsible 2 party
Closed society (exclusive)	Open society (inclusive)
Rule of men	Rule of law
Public rights only (no bill of rights)	Public and private rights (bill of rights)
Irreligious and secularized	More religious - natural or revealed law
Group or states end; Individual means	Individual end; state means
State and society one	Separation of state and society
Controlled communications media	Free communications media
Secret police and torture	Police for internal order

(Continued)

TABLE 3 (Continued)

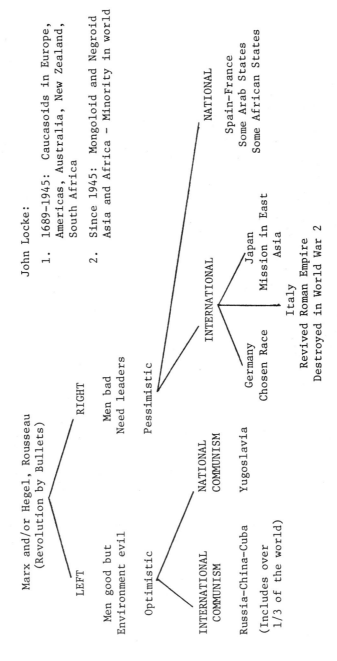

Totalitarianism

Marx and/or Hegel, Rousseau
(Revolution by Bullets)

LEFT

RIGHT

Men good but
Environment evil

Men bad
Need leaders

Optimistic

Pessimistic

INTERNATIONAL
COMMUNISM

NATIONAL
COMMUNISM

INTERNATIONAL

NATIONAL

Russia-China-Cuba
(Includes over
1/3 of the world)

Yugoslavia

Germany
Chosen Race

Japan
Mission in East
Asia

Italy
Revived Roman Empire
Destroyed in World War 2

Spain-France
Some Arab States
Some African States

Democracy

John Locke:

1. 1689-1945: Caucasoids in Europe,
Americas, Australia, New Zealand,
South Africa

2. Since 1945: Mongoloid and Negroid
Asia and Africa - Minority in world

PART II

Electives and Findings Reports

The Preparation of Missionaries to Cope With Political Change

David H. Adeney

In the consideration of our topic, we will consider three areas: Understanding the problems that the church will face, preparing the church now for future political changes, and what should be done after leaving the country.

UNDERSTANDING THE PROBLEMS THAT THE CHURCH WILL FACE

* The demand to cooperate with the government.
  With the "united front" policy, the government in the early days will emphasize freedom of religion and call upon Christians to support the government.

    Question: How far can the church support the
                government when the government actions
                are contrary to Scripture?

    Example: In Ethiopia, some Christians are co-
                operating with the government. Others
                are asking why they do not protest
                against government killings.

* The demand that the church sever all ties with those described as imperialists.
  Christians are required to denounce missionaries. Nationals who have been in close touch with missionaries may be in trouble.

* The attempt to divide the church through the introduction of false teachers and government agents who will

infiltrate Christian organizations and accuse those whose
thinking is not sufficiently "progressive".

* Compulsory indoctrination of all church members with the
constant repetition of a subtle form of scientific materialism which is calculated to undermine faith.
    Two kinds of Christians will be in danger: those who
    lack reality in their experience of Christ, and those
    who, while zealous in their devotional life, are not
    firmly grounded in the knowledge of the Scriptures
    and have not thought through the challenge of
    Communism.

* The system of self-criticism and mutual criticism, which
requires Christians to "struggle against" fellow members
of the body of Christ.

* The ban on all Christian youth activities.
    No religious teaching among young people is permitted,
    though the government cannot control what goes on in
    the home. Children will be taught to denounce their
    parents and report any anti-revolutionary teaching
    given in the home.

* A regimentation of time, making fellowship with other
Christians very difficult and attendance at regular
meetings almost impossible.

* The take-over of all Christian educational, medical, and
social service institutions.

* The suppression of all Christian publications and the
attempt to destroy Bibles.

* The branding of all Christian workers as teachers of
superstition.
    Their full-time ministry in the church will be stopped,
    and they will have to support themselves through
    manual labor.

PREPARING THE CHURCH NOW FOR FUTURE POLITICAL CHANGES

* Withdraw from positions of responsibility in the church
and encourage national leadership.

* Be very sensitive to the feelings of national fellow-
workers, and be prepared to leave when your presence becomes an embarrassment to them.

* Be sure that all property is held in the name of the local church, that all organizations have local names, and that they are not related to foreign institutions.

* Help Christians to understand the sovereignty of God and the significance of the church in His eternal purpose.

* Teach and encourage local Christians so that *they* can prepare and publish a true Christian apologetic with emphasis upon the biblical view of man, of sin, and of salvation in contrast to the Communist views; show how to answer Communist claims with humility, love, and conviction.

* Emphasize the fact that only a church with spiritual depth, fervent love for the Lord and for one another, and dependence upon the power of the Holy Spirit will be able to stand.

* Emphasize the importance of small groups and the use of laymen in the leadership of the church. If necessary, restructure the church organization. If the church is completely dependent upon one person, it will not be prepared to maintain a true witness if the leader is removed.

* Help the church to distinguish between essentials and non-essentials. Teach the true nature of the church, and show how the church can remain even if regular services cannot continue.

* Encourage the formation of small family groups; family loyalty and worship within the home are vitally important.

* Urge members of the church to examine their life style. Are they living a simple life, reaching out to the poor; or are they completely identified with the upper middle class? Christians may have to go to the country where they will have to develop simple skills and work with their hands.

* Develop skills in memorizing and copying the Scriptures, including simple forms of printing.

* Plan a series of bases in the countryside and provide hidden supplies of Scriptures and other helpful books.

* Be sure to keep copies of all books that are published within the country in a safe place outside the country.

* Discuss with national Christians the most helpful type of program to be broadcast from outside radio broadcasts.

AFTER LEAVING THE COUNTRY

* Mobilize prayer support outside the country for Christians in the midst of trial. If possible, develop some form of communication via national Christians who are living abroad and may be able to keep in touch with their brothers and sisters in the country.

* Keep in touch with political and social developments through reading secular reports and books.

* * * *

GROUP FINDINGS REPORT

Missionaries living in politically unstable areas must seek to understand the type of problems they are likely to face if they have to live under an authoritarian government. They must prepare not only themselves, but also the church for radical changes in its life and witness.

The following questions--ones that may arise under a totalitarian regime--were discussed:

   * When called to cooperate with the government, should the church protest against government violation of human rights and biblical principles?

   * What should be the attitude of missionaries when the government demands that the church sever all relations with "imperialists"?

   * How can the church guard against divisive influences and false teaching produced by infiltration of Communist agents?

   * What can be done to prepare Christians to face indoctrination and the necessity to take part in self-criticism?

* How can they avoid criticizing fellow Christians and pre-
serve a real spirit of fellowship?

* What can be done to prepare the church for the time when
many of the regular activities, such as regular Sunday
services, Sunday schools, youth groups, etc., will cease
and Christians face extreme regimentation of their time?

* It was suggested that missionaries should withdraw from
positions of leadership and encourage the churches to
train laymen and arrange for team leadership rather than
depending upon one man.

* The need for the organization of small family groups with
a deep loyalty to Christ and to one another was emphasized. It was proposed that nationals be encouraged, by
all means, to prepare a Christian apologetic that can be
used in a Marxist society.

An important outcome of this elective was the proposal
by many that this material should form the basis of a
manual to assist missionaries in preparing the church for
life in a hostile society.

Prefield Training to Enable Future Missionaries to Cope With Political Change

Walter L. Baker

Reared in an Archie Bunker neighborhood, I was indoctrinated by my father in the 3 R's--religion, race, and Republican politics. Such a background has many subtle implications, supporting an egocentric world view. Unless counteracted, this could lead to a communicator that confuses the implications of the gospel with his own sociopolitical world view. Therefore, prefield training of a cross-cultural communicator takes on larger dimensions because we are not simply dealing with an ideology, but an attitude.

Our question is not new, and Jack Frizen reported it in the spring issue of *Evangelical Missions Quarterly* in 1972 in his article, "Executives Tell Missions Profs What They Think" (p. 145). Missionary candidates were identified as having a:

> Lack of perception in separating out that which is the essence of the gospel and that which is a cultural form of expression. Training that reinforces a middle-class role and suburban packaging of the faith. What is worse is that it is done uncritically and often unknowingly. For a missionary serving in a cross-cultural environment, this is critical.

> Lack of understanding of communicating the gospel in diverse environments. Personal work concept closely identified with witnessing to

strangers, not to friends; comfortable witnessing to the world, but uncomfortable as
friends with those in the world.

Lack of interpersonal coping skills; tendency
to spiritualize simplistic solutions for
emotional human problems and conflicts; in-
adequate understanding of techniques and tools
for handling stress.

What has been done since 1972 to provide a more adequate
prefield training? When and where does it occur? We pro-
pose the following:

1. That prefield training is complex and should begin
   at home and in the church in the formation of a world
   view.

2. That the sooner one is committed to a cross-cultural
   ministry, the more specific the training can be and
   should be.

3. That the mission board is ultimately responsible to
   evaluate and provide for prefield briefing, regarding
   strategy within the various socio-political contexts.

4. That prefield training in the area of politics and
   government is attitudinal rather than purely ideo-
   logical for the cross-cultural communicators; that
   rather than a new course, though one might be helpful,
   certain principles should be communicated to missionaries before they cross political boundaries. Some
   of these principles are:

   * All governments are ordained by God; therefore,
     there is no place for the isolationist.

   * The missionary is a "guest" of the country; there-
     fore, he has no rights, only privileges.

   * The missionary's attitude should be one of observa-
     tion without complaints.

   * The cross-cultural communicator should be able to
     measure differences, but to withhold value
     judgments.

* As an "outsider," he must learn to "live with the
people, love the people, and *learn* from the people,"
as stated by Antonio Nunez of Guatemala.

* The missionary communicator should stimulate the
"insider" to appreciate his heritage and enter into
his country's affairs, desiring to make it the best.

* Mission strategists should be aware of the political climate, and provide guidelines for candidates
and missions, enabling them to work within various
political contexts.

Finally, how do we start? I have these suggestions:

1. The writing of articles and helps for the Christian
home toward the formation of a world view.

2. Guidelines for the integration of media presentations
as teaching aids within the home.

3. The production of teaching materials for churches and
Sunday schools, geared toward an holistic view of the
world and what is going on, related to the educational materials used in schools.

4. The encouragement of pastors to deal with the issues
of the Christian's relationship to government, by
clear exegesis of passages involved.

5. The cooperation of mission leaders to encourage committed students to take those courses that will give
a more adequate preparation for cross-cultural
ministry.

6. The development of courses and internships that will
provide prefield exposure and principles for communication in various socio-political contexts, including
the utilization of input from leaders from these
areas.

7. The preparation of materials by the IFMA, EFMA, and
AEPM toward prefield orientation in the realm of
socio-political environments and how to cope with
them and communicate to them, which would be a prefield requirement.

* * * *

GROUP FINDINGS REPORT

Prefield Training Defined

Preparation of missionaries for service in various socio-
political environments is complex in that it varies with
each individual's world view and that the ultimate place of
ministry is often unknown until formal training has been
completed. Much of his prefield training deals with his
attitudes formed during his life in the area of politics
and/or government. Beginning at home and continuing
throughout the period of education, by church and school,
the final responsibility for education and prefield education rests with the mission board.

Prefield Political Orientation Expected

Before arriving on the field, the board should evaluate
or facilitate:

  1. One's *biblical* posture: in relation to government
     in agreement with the mission's stance.

  2. One's *sociological* posture:

     a. Can he measure the differences in political
        ideology with maturity?
     b. Is he ready not only to live with and love, but
        learn from the receiving people?

  3. One's *political* posture:

     a. By passport and visa, he is a guest with
        privileges.
     b. By birth, the receiving people are citizens
        with rights and obligations to be exercised.

  4. One's *historical* posture: Is he acquainted with the
     why and wherefore of the political context in which
     he will be asked to work?

Practical Suggestions Gleaned

  1. Increased articles and materials that teach principles
     in these areas of concern.

  2. Structured programs in postcandidate school, prefield
     training period, either by the mission or by referral
     to training programs in progress.

3. Preparation of materials for prefield briefings, including the areas of government and relationships to it.

4. The need to update and utilize materials, such as *The Missionary Legal Manual*.

5. The need of a structured first-term program as preservice training.

Aftermath to Persecution

T. Grady Mangham, Jr.

As we look at our topic, *Aftermath to Persecution*, I have chosen to consider two countries: first, Viet Nam; then, Chad.

VIET NAM

Population - North 22,000,000
          South 18,700,000

Religions - (South only)

Buddhist	80.5%	(includes Caodai, Hoa Hao, and ancestor worshippers)
Roman Catholic	10.0%	
Animist	8.0%	
Protestant	1.5%	

The tenth edition of the *Mission Handbook: North American Protestant Ministries Overseas* (1973) listed more than 20 Protestant mission agencies active in Viet Nam. At least seven of these had as one of their principal purposes the establishing of churches. Those church-planting groups listed a total of 166 expatriot personnel, one-half of which were serving with The Christian and Missionary Alliance. By 1975, Protestant churches numbered more than 600; and baptized believers were in excess of 60,000.

Mission Involvement

   My report will have almost exclusively to do with The
Christian and Missionary Alliance involvement. Protestant
mission work began in 1911 during the period when the entire region was known as French Indochina. Personnel were
quickly located in several major cities in the north,
central, and southern parts of what is today the Socialist
Republic of Viet Nam. By 1927, an indigenous church organization (the Evangelical Church of Viet Nam) had been
formed. Rapid growth was experienced until 1941. That
year all missionaries who remained in Viet Nam were interned and remained imprisoned until the end of World War
II. The church carried on alone until 1945.

   The period 1946-1954 was characterized by fighting and
disruption throughout the countryside. The French, seeking
to re-establish their colonial rule, controlled many of the
major cities and some of the highways. The independence
movement was under Communist control. Missionaries and
national Christians were ambivalent about their loyalties.
Many churches and thousands of believers were located in
areas controlled by the Viet Minh. When the Geneva Accords
were signed in 1954, all missionary personnel left North
Viet Nam. Some pastors, church groups, and hundreds of
Christians remained in the North when the Communist government was established there. Some pastors and several
thousand Christians moved to the South.

   The period of 1954 to 1960 was one of relative peace and
much development in South Viet Nam. The mission was very
active, and the church experienced good growth.

   The time from 1960 to 1975 represented a period of
deepening American involvement militarily, intensified terrorism, and increasing military activity.

   The mission/church ministered in 23 different languages
throughout the country. Mission activities included evangelism and church planting, language reduction, Scripture
translation, literature production and distribution, literacy programs, Bible schools and seminary, leprosarium
(including 2 hospitals and 17 village clinics), ·relief
ministries to refugees from terrorism and battle-affected
areas.

Church Situation

In early 1975, the ECVN had assumed the following proportions: 6 districts, including 2 tribal or Montagnard
districts; 550 organized churches; baptized membership of
54,000+; 276 students in full-time theological training;
171 ordained pastors; church-owned and operated press; a
publications office; 2 hospitals; and several clinics. The
church president and 6 district superintendents were totally
supported by the churches, as were all pastors and Bible
school students. In 1974, the church reported 4,128 baptisms. Including the TEE, there were more than 1,500 individuals involved in supervised study of the Scriptures.
There were 37 churches within the city of Saigon. Over the
years, people's movements had occurred among several of the
tribal groupings, the most recent of which had been among
the Stieng where, during the period of 1972-1975 about
15,000 had turned to Christ.

Development Leading to Period of "Persecution"

The church and mission had many indications that the time
might come when the church would live under a Marxist-
oriented government. One could pinpoint only a few of these
as follows:

1. 1941-1945 - World War II and the emergence of the
              Vietnamese Liberation Movement (Viet
              Minh).

2. 1945-1954 - Period of divided loyalties when many
              churches existed within Communist-
              controlled areas.

3. 1954 - Division of the country.

4. 1962 - The leprosarium attacked at Banmethuot, and 3
          mission personnel taken captive.

5. 1965 - The U.S. Embassy attacked with the subsequent
          decision by the mission to move the MK school
          from Dalat to Thailand.

6. 1968 - The TET offensive when 6 missionaries were
          killed and 2 were captured.

7. 1972 - The NVA offensive in the Northern Provinces of
          South Viet Nam.

8. 1975 - The March attack at Banmethuot when 5 mission-
    aries were taken prisoner, and then, of course,
    the subsequent developments.

Preparations by the Mission and/or the Evangelical Church
  of Viet Nam

The church was organized as an indigenous body in 1927
with complete autonomy. In 1941, all mission properties,
including furnishings, were confided to the church leaders
when mission personnel had to leave, or were interned. The
Bible school continued in session. The church paper (*Thanh
Kinh Bao*) was published, and all church ministries continued. When the mission returned in 1945, it was with a
recognition of the church's maturity. Shortly thereafter,
a Vietnamese dean was named to give direction to the Bible
school. A program was instituted for the training of
additional Bible school faculty (overseas scholarships).
Plans were made for the development of a pastor's library
in the Vietnamese language. When a decision was reached
to build a new Bible seminary, it became a joint project--
the church provided the land, and the mission provided the
funds. All funds were turned over to the church, however,
and the church supervised the construction of the seminary.
There was no missionary participation in the administrative
affairs of the church at the local district or national
level. Joint meetings were held periodically between the
church Executive and Mission Committees to coordinate those
areas where church and mission worked in close cooperation.
There was the joint development of a national scale evangelism program called Evangelism Deep and Wide. An effective
TEE program was developed at several academic levels. The
mission consulted with national church leaders regarding
missionaries' role during differing stages of political
developments.

I am sure mistakes were made during the entire period
mentioned above. We were probably too closely identified
with the U.S. government and military presence. However,
most of our contacts with these agencies, or individuals,
were either for spiritual ministries to them or to seek
assistance and benefit for the churches. We probably did
not teach clearly the dangers and/or merits of Marxism.
That is difficult to do under circumstances where a part of
the church is constantly exposed to Communist cadres and
where the government in power could misinterpret any
questionable statements. There are probably other areas
where we failed. I trust there will be freedom to discuss
and to suggest such when the proper time comes.

"Persecution" Examples

The church in Viet Nam has not been singled out for
"persecution" at any point in recent history, to my knowledge. The church and individual Christians have suffered
along with the rest of the population. There may have
been isolated instances of local officials who have vented
personal animosities. There are many instances where
Christians and/or missionaries were killed, or captured, or
were driven from their places of residence. As far as I
know, these were all politically motivated.

The above is not to say that Marxism in Viet Nam em-
braces or encourages Christianity. It is materialistic and
anti-God in its philosophy, and it is bent on making all
elements of society cooperate in achieving its goals. It
will "use" the church if the church agrees to cooperate in
achieving goals, many of which in themselves are good. It
will resist the church, using violent methods if necessary,
if the church stands against what it sees as the forwarding
of its goals and purposes.

Aftermath

All of the C&MA missionaries left Viet Nam in April, 1975.
There were several reasons for this, which may be discussed if desired. Also, approximately 1,600 Christians,
including 35 pastors and/or Bible school students, left at
that time. Subsequent reports reaching us indicated that
there was no adverse reaction regarding the departure of
the missionaries, though the following may be worthy of
note:

1. Church leaders in North Viet Nam have accused the
   C&MA of "abandoning" them since 1954.

2. When MCC representatives visited Viet Nam in July
   this year, a spokesman for the church in the South
   expressed great appreciation for the Mennonite ex-
   patriots who remained in Viet Nam in April, 1975.

May I state that those who have visited Viet Nam since
the country was reunited are unanimous in insisting that
there is religious liberty in Viet Nam, consistent with the
"liberties" in any Marxist-oriented, controlled society;
that is, religion has not been singled out for government
opposition or persecution. But, let us look at what we
know of the church.

First, in the North:

1. The church has succeeded in making an accommodation
   to the government. Leadership emerged that is acceptable to the "party." Some would say the church
   has become politicized.

2. The reports given indicate many more churches and
   more believers than in 1954. It is difficult to
   assess the accuracy of such reports. Attendance at
   the one church in Hanoi, from which there have been
   reports on several occasions, runs between 40 and 60.
   The church appears to be active.

3. Church leaders in the North do not admit to any restrictions. They reportedly have Sunday school,
   worship services, evangelistic services, prayer
   meeting and Bible study, and youth meetings. There
   are reports of additions to the church, baptisms,
   and sessions for the training of ministerial
   candidates.

Next, in the South:

1. A change of leadership, brought about after a government spokesman suggested this would enhance the
   church's image, resulted in an elderly Christian
   statesman's being chosen to fill that role. Without
   doubt, this can only be viewed as a transition. A
   younger man, more acceptable to the "party," is
   recognized by the government as an official liaison
   agent.

2. Institutions formerly operated by the church, such as
   orphanages, schools, and clinics, have been taken
   over by the government.

3. The Bible seminary, permitted to continue its program
   of ministerial training during the 1975-1976 school
   year, has since been closed.

4. No church conferences at either the district or regional level have been permitted since early 1977.

5. Publication of Christian literature has been strictly
   controlled, and open-air evangelism, and even house-
   to-house witnessing, have been forbidden.

6. Unconfirmed reports indicate that listening to out-of-country radio is prohibited. The paucity of response to the programs from FEBC would seem to corroborate this.

7. Some churches are reported to have been closed. A figure mentioned from several sources is 90.

8. Some pastors have been "detained" and sent to "re-education camps." Several sources mention approximately 100. Reasons given for this have been: some served as chaplains in the South Viet Nam forces; some tribal pastors were involved in FULRO (a political movement among the tribal groups for autonomy); and a few preached prophetic messages concerning Christ's coming and the destruction of Russia.

9. There are reports of close surveillance on all individuals, and also of enforced moves by some to "new economic zones."

But many churches are meeting, with various activities reported; that is, Sunday school, worship, evangelistic services, special occasions, and baptisms. Also, there are reports from both the North and the South of church buildings repaired or rebuilt with funds from "The Fatherland Front."

There are also reports of negotiations toward eventually reuniting the churches in both North and South.

CHAD

The total population of the country - 4,000,000

Religions represented: Muslim   - 52%
                        Animist   - 43%
                        Protestant   - 3%
                        Roman Catholic - 2%

The tenth edition of the *Mission Handbook*, published in 1973, listed five Protestant groups serving in Chad, with a total of 73 expatriot personnel. Protestant missions entered the country in 1920. The population in the northern two-thirds of the country is sparse and predominately Arab-related. More than half of the population lives in the southern third of the country, and the church has grown

more rapidly here. When trouble broke out in late 1972 and
during 1973, the total number of churches of all groups
exceeded 1,500, with more than 60,000 members.

I received specific information only from TEAM Mission,
one of the two major Protestant groups. TEAM's involvement
began only in 1969 when they effected a merger with the
Sudan United Mission, North America Branch. The work of
SUM had begun in 1926 while the area was still a part of
French Equatorial Africa. In 42 years, the work had grown
to 258 self-governing and self-supporting churches, with an
additional 163 meeting places, and a total baptized membership of 42,000.

The Evangelical Church in Chad (TEAM) was working with 6
different language groups. It was estimated that only 3 per
cent of the population in this area was literate. Mission
activities included language reduction, Scripture translation, literature production, literacy programs, a press and
7 bookstores, a hospital and a maternity clinic, several
dispensaries where ministry was carried on among people
afflicted with leprosy, a French-language theological
school, and several Bible schools in vernacular languages.

Most congregations in the Evangelical Church in Chad
were directed by lay leaders. There was an intensive program to train leaders for all branches of the work in the
church.

The government of President Ngarta Tombalbaye began to
experience difficulty shortly after Chad received independence. A Southerner, the President had most of his support
in the South. The northern two-thirds of the country was
plagued by an unpublicized civil war, and gradually it fell
under the control of rebels. In an effort to bolster his
political position, the President launched a "cultural
revolution." All European influence was to be removed. All
non-Chadean names had to be changed. A presidential decree
ordered that all tribesmen must submit to traditional initiation rites--secret ceremonies often involving sacrifice
to ancestral spirits, circumcision, and an animistic
"re-birth."

President Tombalbaye was born into a Baptist family in
1918 and became a leader and teacher in the Baptist Church.
He was also one of the founders of a nationalist political
group which agitated for independence from the French.
When the Church disciplined him for un-Christian behavior,

Tombalbaye became bitter and blamed the local Baptist missionary. The President also had not been happy with the
Baptists for using the Sango language among his own Sara
tribe prior to independence in 1960. Some felt, therefore,
that he was at least partially prompted in his program and
in his subsequent harsh reaction to the Church by personal
bitterness. In addition to the above, some felt they de-
tected a pro-Arab move on the part of the President, doubt-
less in an effort to relieve pressure from the Muslim
rebels.

As government officials sought to enforce the President's
order, and began to round up men and boys to take them to
secret camps in the forest for the initiation rites,
Christians protested; and the stage was set for confrontation between church and state. One evangelist declared,
"The Lord has commanded us not to worship sun, or stone, or
tree. So, we have told the President and his men that we
will worship only the Living God, even if they kill us."
The subject was discussed by church leaders, and the
idolatrous aspects of the process were brought to light.
Some Christians, under threat by government authority, submitted to the initiation rites. When disciplinary action
was discussed in a local Baptist church, the members voted
not to discipline those taken by threat or force. One of
the missionaries presented the scriptural view of the question as he saw it, and another vote was taken, which over-
turned the first. During November of 1973, missionaries of
Baptist missions were asked to leave the country. Some
were arrested and held in prison even before they could de-
part, but they were later permitted to leave.

Some Baptist pastors who were leaders in the churches
and who had fearlessly expressed their opposition to the
initiation rites were arrested. The Baptist mission and
its churches were declared dissolved. Two renegade pastors,
chosen by the President, were declared the only recognized
leaders of the new church, which was to be called "Chaddean
Evangelical Church." All Baptist pastors were then asked
to accept his new organization, and with it, accept the
cultural revolution, which included the initiation. Many
leaders signed under duress. Some refused. Those who refused were imprisoned and subjected to harsh treatment.
Later it was learned that those who stedfastly refused were
murdered, and their bodies buried in unmarked graves.

Leaders of the Evangelical Church in Chad (TEAM) re-
quested the missionaries to say nothing officially on the

question of initiation. If pressed, they were to reply
that they were not in a position to say what was involved
and that they should refer government officials to the
church leaders for any answer. Though some of the missionaries had serious questions about this, the church leaders
insisted and assured the missionaries that they were ready
to suffer and that they would take a stand when the time
came, and would not capitulate even if it cost them their
lives. Warnings were given to missionaries that officials
were visiting churches to listen in to messages, and the
leaders pled that nothing be said that could make things
harder for the church. As pressure began to mount within
the area where the Evangelical Church of Chad (TEAM) was
located, some pastors were reported to have advised
Christians to go rather than get killed. Others told their
people to submit because of the terrible consequences if
they did not. It became clear that the church was taking
no concerted stand and that any resistance would come from
individual churches or individual Christians.

Isolated cases of valiant attempts to resist initiation
were reported. Stories of terrible atrocities began cir-
culating, too. Pastors were buried alive, and everything
taken from their families. One pastor was put into a big
drum and his protruding feet tied to a tree where he suffered many days until he was finally strangled. Another
had his fingers broken one by one in an effort to make him
succumb. An aged pastor was forced to go to the camp where
he got out his Bible and preached. A quick blow on the back
of his neck ended his sermon and his life. Others were tied
together hand and foot and thrown into the river. Stories
of people buried alive with one foot sticking out as a
warning to others continued to be reported.

An elder in one of the churches, and also a government
employee, wrote a letter entitled, "Boundary between the
realm of Caesar and that of God," which stated the biblical
position on initiation and encouraged Christians to resist
it to death. Many pastors and evangelists read this letter
in their public services. Others feared its implications
and refused to read it.

When an employee of the Mission Church hospital was
forcefully taken to initiation, and the pastor's appeal did
no good, the doctors closed the hospital for a week. A
personal representative of the President flew down to endeavor to patch things up. They did not want the hospital
closed. This individual tried to make the pastor the

scapegoat; but when the doctors supported him, he was not
arrested. The pastor had taken a strong stand against
initiation, openly stating his convictions.

Those Christians who submitted to the initiation rites
were resented by the Christians who had resisted. In turn,
the initiated Christians tried to justify their actions.
The government got involved when it told the initiated
Christians that they were free to take up their Christian
activities again. Local pastors were called before government officials and told to reinstate the pastors, elders,
and church officials in their former tasks and positions.
Some pastors did this. Missionaries no longer felt free to
fellowship with these groups, and in some areas it was difficult to find a group who maintained its integrity. Some
church leaders insisted on public repentance and confession
of sin before anyone was allowed back into fellowship.
Former leaders were accepted into church fellowship, but
were not permitted to take up their positions of leadership
as elders, Sunday school teachers, etc.

On April 13, 1975, a military coup overthrew President
Tombalbaye's government. Many political prisoners were
released, and the names of those who had died in prison were
published. The new government assured freedom of religion
and said the state would be secular and not religious. All
laws restricting religious groups were repealed. Initiation
could be practiced by those who wished it, but it would not
be forced upon any.

In the church, people were much relieved, and there was
great rejoicing--but how to unravel the past? After the
coup, a group of men wrote a circular letter asking all
leaders who had gone to initiation to resign their posts for
at least a year as a sign of repentance and humility. Six
of the men were members of the Central Church Executive
Committee. The rest were representatives of the various
regions. The letter was well received in most areas, but in
some places those who had "repented" objected forcefully. A
spirit of division developed within the church, which became
a serious problem, and a stumbling block to spiritual
growth and development.

In 1975, one of the missionaries asked, "What are the
lessons of all these very discouraging experiences? First,
that too many of our Christians, even the leaders, were not
ready to stand for truth and convictions in face of persecution and death.... Second, our people are not grounded

in the Word. It has often been repeated that the church is growing numerically much faster than it is growing in knowledge and spiritual discernment, and this was again underlined. Thirdly, our churches seem to have failed in 'little' questions of conscience, and this prepared the way to spiritual defeat."

In a letter dated March 8, 1976, one of the TEAM missionaries wrote: "The leaders who had taken a firm stand felt that the ones who had compromised themselves lacked the moral and spiritual force to lead the great effort that was necessary to purify and strengthen the church that was almost mortally wounded; yet the compromised leaders held onto their positions as hard as they could. Satan had failed to destroy the church by external force, but it seemed now that he was succeeding by internal division and strife.

"We missionaries were in a dilemma. We wanted to speak out to tell the church that new leaders must be elected, but we felt absolutely no implusion from the Holy Spirit to do so. In fact, the more we prayed, the more we were led just to wait upon God; so we did just what we were led to do, and no more. We prayed for the church in her hour of crisis." He then related what took place at the General Assembly of the church during the month of January. A true spirit of revival, of brokenness, and of repentance was evident. The letter continued, "We feel that we have learned a great lesson through these experiences. We humans are very prone to act when we see a need, whether the Holy Spirit is leading us or not. Had we yielded to the impulse to speak out before the General Assembly, we would never have known what great blessing God wanted to bring upon the church in His own time and in His own way."

* * * *

GROUP FINDINGS REPORT

Persecutions in Chad, Viet Nam, and Ethiopia have given missions some guidelines for future conduct, priority, policy, and ministry in these and possibly other lands.

Key Points

1. Some national pastors left in Viet Nam were "re-educated" by the government after the missionaries left.

2. Many pastors in Chad during time of persecution were lay people with very little training.

3. Missionaries in Chad who spoke out against government were asked by the government to leave.

4. Missionaries in Viet Nam were advised by the church leaders to leave because of threat and embarrassment.

5. The church in Viet Nam understood clearly the "how" of living under a Communist regime.

6. Missionaries had open and unrestrained contacts with the U.S. military and Government personnel. This seemed to be unwise and placed them under suspicion.

Suggestions for Action

1. Withdraw before takeover, as missionaries would not be able to minister later and would become an embarrassment to local church leaders.

2. More emphasis should be placed on small cell meetings.

3. Little or no contact with U.S. Government and military lest, in the eyes of the government, missionary and U.S. Government become synonymous.

4. An intensive overall Bible training program, as well as an intensive one for pastors, is' essential to strengthen the doctrinal understanding of the people.

5. A policy of silence on the part of the missionary concerning Communism and government.

The Role of Legitimacy of Government and the Problem of Anarchy

George W. Peters

Government is a divine institution. Even though the Bible does not inform us specifically of the beginning of the order, Paul tells us that government is ordained by God (Romans 13:1) and that government is the minister of God (13:4, 6). Paul adds three descriptive phrases to his statements and says: The government is for good, to avenge evil, and has the authority to receive tribute. The latter words remind us of the words of Peter, who writes in a very similar vein (I Peter 2:13-17).

The New Testament does not reflect negatively upon government as an institution, although Herod falls under the judgment of John the Baptist (Luke 3:19, 20); Christ speaks of Herod as a fox (Luke 13:32); and according to Acts 12:20-23, Herod was smitten of the Lord and died of a dreadful disease. The New Testament thus seems to allow us, in our evaluation, to differentiate between government as an institution and men who occupy the seat of authority.

The Christians are exhorted to:

1. "Render to Caesar the things that are Caesar's" (Mark 12:17).

2. Pay to the government their tribute (Romans 13:6).

3. Be subject to the powers (Romans 13:1; I Peter 2:13).

4. Do honor to the government (I Peter 2:17).

5. Pray for the government (I Timothy 2:1, 2).

Deductions

1. The legitimacy of the government may be deduced from
   three sources:

   a. The Bible speaks of the government as a divine
      order; it is ordained by God.
   b. It is reasonable that God as the Governor of
      the universe and the God of order would insti-
      tute human government for orderly procedure
      and progress.
   c. Human society, such as it is, demands govern-
      ment for an orderly and safe life.

   Thus, history, reason, and the Bible support the
   legitimacy of government.

2. Paul describes the role of government as threefold:

   a. To seek, support, and advance that which is
      good.
   b. To provide conditions for an orderly and peace-
      ful life (I Timothy 2:2).
          On several occasions, Paul called upon the
          government for his rights, for protection,
          and for his advantage (Acts 16:37-39;
          22:25-29; 25:10-12).
   c. To execute wrath upon him that does evil.

These are very comprehensive concepts. They express
moral value judgments of far-reaching effects and are determined by the world and life view of the authorities. It
is here where the responsibility of Christians is entering
the scene. The Christians are to be the light of the world
and the salt of the earth (Matthew 5:13-16); their teaching,
presence, example, and influence must be made to count.
They are to pray for the government and expect God to move
in history. There may come times and circumstances when the
Christians must passively resist the orders of the government, whatever the consequences may be. Bound in their
conscience, they assert with the apostles: "We must obey
God rather than man" (Acts 4:19; 5:29). It is on this
principle that the "underground church" functions, ready to
suffer for it. It is also this principle that has been used
to justify "smuggling" of Bibles and Christian literature
into countries behind the "iron curtain." I am prepared to
leave this to the conscience of the individual without ex-
pressing moral judgment on it. My serious question is:
Have we honestly explored all legal ways to help our

brethren and churches? People who cannot answer this question in the positive should not harshly judge men who follow byways.

I draw attention to two serious misapplications of Scripture. The first is the practice of carrying over Old Testament theocratic principles into modern democracy. This is a misuse of Scripture. Present-day governments are not a continuation of Old Testament theocratic principles as given to Israel. While we may learn from them and strive towards such ideals, democracy is not theocracy. Democracy is man's rule, and not God's rule. Our governments are the continuation of the governments of the non-Jewish nations of the Old Testament--we hope, however, somewhat savored by Christian influences and idealism.

The second error relates to the exposition of such passages as Ephesians 6:12 and Colossians 2:15. It is not uncommon to apply these passages to governments and other human establishments. A proper exegesis does not justify such. While it may be true that Satan in his demonic devices seeks to incarnate himself in men and human institutions, this is not necessarily so. We have no more right to indiscriminately apply this to governments than to religion and ecclesiasticism or other establishments.

Just a word about anarchy. Anarchy prevails when there is no government to enforce law and order. I have gone through several years of it after the Russian revolution in 1917 and in the years of the civil war. It may be described as a time of utter chaos and total lawlessness, a time when might triumphs completely over right, when each man is a law to himself and his own defender. Almost any government is better than no government, and anarchy can only be described as the horror of mankind. It may be the judgment of God in the hands of evil, brutal, and destructive men.

* * * *

GROUP FINDINGS REPORT

The family, church, and state are divinely ordained institutions. However, the Old Testament theocracy is not transferrable to the present. The role of government is to restrain by police. Emphasis is needed on positive reform for the public welfare. Evangelicals fall short when it comes to pressure for reform as the salt of the earth.

Governments have the right to control property and money, conscript manpower, and arrange civil law. They have no right to control the spiritual life of subjects. Christians may adopt passive resistance in matters of conscience. They may seek reform through awakening public awareness, exerting pressure by legitimate political means.

Any form of government is to be preferred to anarchy.

Summary

* Non-violent resistance should not lead to violence.

* The Christian's response to repression is prayer and fasting.

* Missionaries are guests and must not engage in political activity. The missionary's role is preaching - teaching - helping. Let the Word produce change.

Special Problems Under Totalitarianism

Earle E. Cairns

Constant, accelerating, irresistible, and pervasive
social change is a fact of twentieth century life in the
areas of technology, knowledge explosion, rising expecta-
tions, ethics, and even in religion. Social change is re-
construction of institutions and culture to correct social
imbalance. It offers many problems for missions, including:

1. Increasingly powerful secular state, which may be
   neutral or hostile to religion.
   This creates the problem of power without the balance of a sound mind and love (II Timothy 1:7).
   This is true of states whose revolutions have been
   utopian.

   a. Democratic states, through warfare-welfare allied.
      with nationalism, have become increasingly power-
      ful; and missions, as well as religion in general,
      have come under restrictions.

   b. Mass totalitarian states of the left and right
      either ban or limit the proclamation of the gospel
      and in many cases seem almost to be demonic in
      their demands for total allegiance on the part of
      their subjects.

      * Communist totalitarian states separate church
        and state. At best, they have only a limited
        toleration of Christians, and they ban mission-
        aries. Over one-third of the world's population
        is in such states. The use of the airwaves,

correspondence courses, and possible vocational
missions offer the only means of proclaiming the
gospel.

* Rightist totalitarian states, such as the German
  racist state under Hitler and the Italian im-
  perialist state of Mussolini, have regimented
  religion and tried to make it the servant of the
  state.

* Of the 158 nations in the world in 1976, 65 have
  hardly any civil rights and 53 are partially
  free. Only one-quarter of the world's population is in 40 countries which allow full freedom.

* Missionaries must be trained to live under--and
  cope with--whatever possible ways are available
  to engage in proclamation.

2. Nationalism in the sovereign national state
   Nationalism is an emotional feeling of kinship of
   people in a territory which is based on real or
   imagined common interests.

   a. Ecclesiastical nationalism links religion with the
      national state.

      * The Islamic link with the Afghanistan state has
        led to a ban on missions.

      * Buddhism allied with the state has banned mis--
        sionaries in Ceylon and Burma.

   b. Cultural nationalism may lead to separatist--and
      in some cases, heretical--churches tied in with
      cultural nationalism.

      * Perhaps missionary paternalism is partly to
        blame. Africa has 6,000 church groups, with
        about 7 million people from 34 African countries
        and 290 tribes in such groups, apart from mis-
        sion churches or the regular denominations.

   c. Nationalism may lead to a life style isolated from
      the nationals on the part of the missionaries.

      * Christian hospitality alone would ban such
        isolation (Romans 12:13; Hebrews 13:2; III John
        6, 8).

3. Persecution by the state involving the future of the
   church in totalitarian states.

Missionaries have an obligation to prepare the
church for this.

a. National leadership must be trained in Bible memorization, biblical content, and theology for a
   time when the Bible may be banned.

b. Nationals should be allowed to take over leadership as fast as they can be fitted to do so. Missions should promote national leadership.

c. Christian philosophy of history should be developed
   to encourage people facing antichrist in the demonic state--that in suffering they have the hope
   of Christ's coming (II Timothy 3 and 4).

d. Missionaries should leave when urged to do so by
   the State Department (at least the women and the
   children), when a gospel ministry is banned, and
   when staying would harm the church.

e. The church in persecution could engage in:

   * Respectful apology or dialog if permitted.
   * Flight in some cases.
   * Martyrdom if clearly in the permissive will of
     God.
   * The development of a low profile through house
     churches or cell groups.
   * Remembering the promise of Matthew 28:30.

4. The development of a clear idea of the role of the
   church as not retreat, reform, or revolution, but
   rather renovation based upon these ideas:

   a. *Kerygma* - witness Christ in word, life, and deed
               (I Corinthians 15:3-4; Acts 17:2-3).

   b. *Diakonia* - social service growing out of Christian
                love (Galatians 6:10) - In this way the
                church will be light and salt to
                society.

   c. *Koinonia* - fellowship growing out of worship and
                teaching of the Word in discipling.

   d. *Elpis* - a hope of Christ's coming that keeps one
             from either pessimism or utopianism and
             leads to a realism that seeks proximate
             solutions to the ills of society while
             occupying until Christ comes.

5. The problem of ethical principles in such situations
   as smuggling Bibles, using the airwaves, and entering
   countries for vocational purposes but with the in-
   tention of preaching the gospel.
       A policy of honesty when information is demanded
       is essential, but one need not divulge information
       not demanded.

Our conclusion to this topic, "Special Problems Under
Totalitarianism," is: Whatever the problems, the lordship
of Christ should be held high.

* * * *

GROUP FINDINGS REPORT

World missions must not retreat from the fact that one-
third of the world lives under leftist totalitarian regimes,
and millions of others are under rightist regimes or some
limited forms of democracy. Social and cultural change is
constant and pervasive. Missions must determine strategy
and methods for penetrating all of these.

Where missionaries cannot enter, alternative methods of
penetration should be re-examined; and if possible, im-
proved. Where missionaries can enter, they must be prepared in character, knowledge, and discipline to function
within the country.

By all means, the missionary must avoid political action
and involvement and any effort to change political
structures.

A Church Under
a Socialistic Regime

*NOTE: The author and the editors felt it
was not in the best interest of the
church in Country X to publish the
elective paper; instead, a brief
summary is given.*

The case study of Country X was used to show how a
church exists and has expanded under a totalitarian Marxist
regime. The events that led up to Country X's becoming a
socialistic state, the constitutional provisions, the one
political party's dominance, the president's role in party
and government, his many purges of supposed plotters and
the assistance (through economic aid and technical personnel from Russia, China, Cuba, and Eastern European
nations) are recounted in order to expose the environment
in which the church carries on its work. How evangelical
Christians--while making clear by both word and conduct
that they are loyal, patriotic citizens--have not compromised Christian convictions, have overcome some hindrances, weathered irritations, and have experienced growth
is detailed. There is also an account of one Protestant
mission's being permitted to keep half its missionary
staff in the country when all other missionaries were expelled. The case study ends with guidelines for missionaries working under a totalitarian socialistic government,
including:

1. An ambassador of Christ should not endeavor to promote his ideas of democracy and capitalism.

2. He should fully know the political and social problems and accept the possibility of danger and
   conflict.

3. Though living under a socialistic-Marxist regime,
   the Lord's servant should not try to undermine or
   overthrow it.

4. The missionary must find ways to minister within the
   sphere of freedom offered by the government.

The chief suggestions made during discussions were:

1. The church can survive and grow in the midst of persecution and repression.

2. When a government orders missions to leave the country, options should be explored for some form of continued ministry.

3. Since both church and mission will have difficulties
   working under totalitarian governments, it would help
   if the missions did not have a paternalistic relationship with the national church.

4. The discussion group would like EFMA-IFMA member
   bodies to follow Scriptural principles of church-
   mission relations.

5. The group also recommends that EFMA-IFMA executive
   bodies consider setting up a system of accountability
   reporting by member bodies concerning implementation
   of principles of Scriptural independence of the
   national church.

Is Foreign Mission Neutrality a Myth?

Howard A. Whaley

Mission societies and missionaries have frequently assumed that because they do not become involved in political
issues in the host country, they are, in fact--and perceived
as--neutral by national interests. That assumption needs
to be tested. There are, of course, no simple or single
answers to fit all circumstances. No one proposition is
universally applicable. Several focus on various considera-
tions which are factors in understanding the other's per-
ception of the missionary guest in a host country.

Format

In this workshop, we will work through together a
General Thesis and a number of *Propositions* designed to
focus on different aspects of the issue in order to vali-
date or invalidate our assumptions about neutrality in a
given situation.

Thesis

Whether the expatriate missionary is or is not viewed
as politically neutral by the government or anti-government
interests in the host country will depend upon a combina-
tion of local factors interpreted according to local per-
ceptions, fears, and biases.

Propositions

1. The missionary (and mission agency) is considered
   "foreign" by neighbors and the host government, no

matter how well he believes himself to be culturally
adjusted.

2. Political realities (polarization, etc.) in many host
   countries do not accommodate neutral or uncommitted
   positions.

3. In developing or politically unstable countries, a
   foreigner provides an alien presence easily identified by all sides of a particular issue, any of which
   may distrust him and/or seek to legitimatize their
   position by soliciting support, or use him as a
   visible symbol of opposition.

4. The missionary is viewed as a foreign "change agent"
   since he is an expatriate whose presence is for the
   purpose of establishing a movement or institution
   imported into the country.

5. Change agents of whatever sort are suspect, even if
   only to determine their true motivation.

6. The non-Christian will find it very difficult to
   understand that the Christian missionary is present
   in his country at a time of crisis for purely al-
   truistic reasons. Therefore, he may assign other
   motives to the missionary.

7. Counter forces will seek to use the missionary and
   the institution he is associated with to their own
   advantage, which may put the missionary in an untenable position with regard to neutrality.

8. The missionary may often be forced to actually com-
   promise--or appear to compromise--his principles
   because, although his sympathies lie with the masses,
   he, of necessity, must comply with and support the
   government.

9. No matter how careful the missionary is, the national
   group/groups are not likely to interpret his inten-
   tions and actions as the missionary assumes they will.

When is it Legitimate to Disobey Government Edicts?

W. Elwyn Davies

I begin with the assumption that the Scriptures, being the Word of God, are adequate to answer the query. God is not caught by surprise by twentieth century developments, whether in the material, political, moral, or spiritual realm. By giving us His Word, God has provided us with a way to discern His will, and this covers every area of the life of a Christian in this world. We are not dependent on human ingenuity, but rather on divine principles clearly enunciated in the Scriptures. With this in mind, *four basic factors* form the foundation for our answer to the question.

The Sovereignty of God

We cannot treat this as a cold, transcendent fact that excites the intellect but leaves us untouched in our daily lives. As citizens of two worlds, we are called upon to "Render...unto Caesar the things that are Caesar's; and unto God the things that are God's" (Matthew 22:21). This is not a matter of "either...or," but of "both...and."

This sovereign God reveals Himself to us in terms of His:

1. *Eternal Purposes*. God's desire for man is not an expression of His response to man's sin and consequent misery. "He chose us in him (Christ) before the creation of the world to be holy and blameless in his sight" (Ephesians 1:4, NIV).

Further light is directed to the question by Paul's
reference to rulers and authorities in the heavenly
realms. He says that "God's intent was that now,
through the church, the manifold wisdom of God should
be made known to the rulers and authorities in the
heavenly realms, according to his eternal purpose
which he accomplished in Christ Jesus our Lord"
(Ephesians 3:10-11, NIV).

It is evident that in the Scriptures we have the
eternal plans of God for man revealed. These plans
are not emergency measures taken by a diety when
caught unprepared by the sin of man; no event on
earth has ever surprised God.

2. *Ordaining of Human Government.* Within the context of
the eternal purposes of God, we have the establish-
ment by God of the principle of human government on
earth. Knowing all that would transpire in terms of
sin and rebellion of restrictive and punitive legis-
lation aimed at the life and liberty of His people,
God still established human authority in the world,
and commanded man to obey it. Thus we have Romans
13:1-7, NIV:

> Everyone must submit himself to the governing
> authorities, for there is no authority except
> that which God has established. The authori-
> ties that exist have been established by God.
> Consequently, he who rebels against the au-
> thority is rebelling against what God has in-
> stituted, and those who do so will bring
> judgment on themselves. For rulers hold no
> terror for those who do right, but for those
> who do wrong. Do you want to be free from
> fear of the one in authority? Then do what is
> right and he will commend you. For he is God's
> servant to do you good. But if you do wrong,
> be afraid, for he does not bear the sword for
> nothing. He is God's servant and agent of
> wrath to bring punishment on the wrongdoer.
> Therefore, it is necessary to submit to the
> authorities, not only because of possible pun-
> ishment but also because of conscience. This
> is also why you pay taxes, for the authorities
> are God's servants, who give their full time
> to governing. Give everyone what you owe him:
> if you owe taxes, pay taxes; if revenue, then

revenue; if respect, then respect; if honor, then honor.

Peter defied the edict of the "rulers and elders" of the Jewish people because he saw it as a direct contradiction of the command of the Lord Jesus to preach "in His name." Acts 4:18-20: "Then they called them in again and commanded them not to speak or teach at all in the name of Jesus. But Peter and John replied 'Judge for yourselves whether it is right in God's sight to obey you rather than God. For we cannot help speaking about what we have seen and heard.'" Later he repeated his defiance and "having brought the apostles, they made them appear before the Sanhedrin to be questioned by the high priest. 'We gave you strict orders not to teach in this name,' he said. 'Yet you have filled Jerusalem with your teaching and are determined to make us guilty of this man's blood.' Peter and the other apostles replied: 'We must obey God rather than men! The God of our fathers raised Jesus from the dead - whom you have killed by hanging him on the tree. God exalted him to his own right hand as Prince and Savior that he might give repentance and forgiveness of sins to Israel. We are witnesses of these things, and so is the Holy Spirit, whom God has given to those who obey him.'" (Acts 5:27-32, NIV). Even Gamaliel recognized the possibility that the Sanhedrin might be "fighting against God" (verse 39).

Yet, in his first letter Peter writes:

> Live such good lives among the pagans that, though they accuse you of doing wrong, they may see your good deeds and glorify God on the day he visits us. Submit yourselves for the Lord's sake to every authority instituted among men: whether to the king, as the supreme authority, or to governors, who are sent by him to punish those who do wrong and to commend those who do right. For it is God's will that by doing good you should silence the ignorant talk of foolish men. Live as free men, but do not use your freedom as a cover-up for evil; live as servants of God. Show proper respect to everyone: love the brotherhood of believers, fear God, honor the king (I Peter 2:12-17, NIV).

Obviously Peter taught believers to obey human governments, and to do so "for the Lord's sake" (verse 13).
The honor of God was at stake.

3. *Unfolding of Human History.* The book of Daniel and
the book of the Revelation are classic examples of
the relationship of a sovereign God to human history
as it unfolds on earth. Daniel insists that, "No wise
man, enchanter, magician or diviner can explain to the
king the mystery he has asked about, but there is a
God in heaven who reveals mysteries." (NIV) He is the
Ultimate Ruler in all human affairs, and in the book
of the Revelation He is on the throne, bringing to
their consummation all the eternal purposes which have
ever been in His heart.

The Responsibility of Man

God made man in His own image (Genesis 1:27), and today
God is at work in the lives of men that they may be "con-
formed to the image of his Son" (Romans 8:29). In between
lies the whole plan of redemption, including the responsibilities laid on the shoulders of man.

Grace was never intended to cancel out human responsibility. Man is still called upon to exert himself to:

1. *Obey the Word of God.* We must always keep in mind the
dignity of a human being, given by God the awesome
privilege of certain (limited) freedoms. This same
Word of God that expresses the absoluteness of God's
sovereignty in Isaiah 45:1-7 also declares man's
freedom in II Timothy 2:20-21: "In a large house
there are articles not only of gold and silver, but
also of wood and clay; some are for noble purposes
and some for ignoble. *If a man cleanses himself* from
the latter, he will be an instrument for noble purposes, made holy, useful to the Master and prepared to
do any good work." Here it is not "Lord, cleanse me,"
but "Lord, I choose to cleanse myself" (cf. Psalm
119:9).

2. *Witness to the Grace of God.* "God has chosen to make
known among the Gentiles the glorious riches of this
mystery, which is Christ in you, the hope of glory"
(Colossians 1:27, NIV). This is the choice of God.
How is it to be done? Paul says, *"We proclaim him,*
counselling and teaching everyone with all wisdom, so

that *we may present* everyone perfect in Christ. To
this end *I labor*, struggling with all the energy he
so powerfully works in me. I want you to know how
strenuously *I am exerting myself* for you" (Colossians
1:28–2:1, NIV).

3. *Participate in the Edification of the Church of God.*
   Completing the church, the body of Christ, is the
   divine goal in this age. To this end the Holy Spirit
   was sent, and the Lord Jesus intercedes without ceas-
   ing. But the responsibility of the believer is also
   clear:

   > It was he who gave some to be apostles, some to
   > be prophets, some to be evangelists, and some
   > to be pastors and teachers, *to prepare God's
   > people for works of service*, so that the body
   > of Christ may be built up until we all reach
   > unity in the faith and in the knowledge of
   > the Son of God and become mature, attaining
   > to the full measure of perfection found in
   > Christ. Then we will no longer be infants,
   > tossed back and forth by the waves, and blown
   > here and there by every wind of teaching and
   > by the cunning and craftiness of men in their
   > deceitful scheming. Instead, speaking the
   > truth in love, we will in all things grow up
   > into him who is the Head, that is, Christ.
   > From him the whole body, joined and held to-
   > gether by every supporting ligament, *grows
   > and builds itself up in love, as each part
   > does its work* (Ephesians 4:11–16, NIV).

The Areas of Apparent Conflict

There are two apparently conflicting areas here:

1. *What the Scriptures Say*
   a. We must give to Caesar what is Caesar's and to God
      what is God's (Matthew 22:21).
   b. We must proclaim Christ to all (Acts 1:8).
   c. We must not forsake the fellowship of the saints
      (Hebrews 10:25).
   d. We must abstain from all appearance of evil
      (I Thessalonians 5:22).

2. *What Our Eyes See*

   a. The claim of totalitarian states to dominate the whole of man.

   b. Human decrees that inhibit the proclamation of the gospel.

   c. Laws aimed at preventing believers from gathering for prayer, worship, and mutual edification.

   d. Regulations that appear to force believers to become involved in situations and practices which are contrary to the Christian ethic.

Are they in conflict?

Specifically: Is a sovereign God likely to state a position in relation to human government that is rendered untenable by the course of history? Will He commission the Church/Christian to act in a manner that conflicts with the injunctions of Scripture?

The Importance of Exactness

Believing as I do in the verbal inspiration of the Scriptures, I am locked into a position in relation to the interpretation of Scripture. *Exactness*, as far as is humanly possible, is demanded of me. Some pertinent questions now come to our attention.

When confronted with issues arising out of real or apparent conflicts between the Word of God and government edicts, I must ask:

1. Does the Bible really say so –
   or is it my (traditional) interpretation?

2. Is this what the Bible commands –
   or has it been modified when filtered through my personality?

3. *Does the Bible direct specifically in this matter* –
   or is there a viable alternative?
   For instance, the Bible directs us to witness and to give the message of salvation to all men. Some countries do not permit open-air preaching or tract distribution. Are there viable alternatives available? Can we use radio from outside the country, or can we witness personally and privately?

4. Do I properly understand the edicts?

Summation

It is legitimate for a Christian to disobey government edicts –

if/when   it is demonstrated that the Christian is specifi-
           cally directed by the Scriptures to follow a cer-
           tain course of action,

or   when the total teaching of the Scriptures clearly
           indicates the will of God in the matter,

while   the edict is in clear contradiction to the teach-
           ing and the directives of the Word of God,

and   to obey the edict will bring him in direct con-
           flict with the Scriptures.

* * * *

GROUP FINDINGS REPORT

Four Basic Factors to be Considered:

1. The sovereignty of God.

   * He ordained human government.

2. The responsibility of man:

   * To obey the Word of God.
   * To live a holy life.
   * To proclaim the Good News.

3. The apparent conflict between the injunction of
   Scripture, e.g., Romans 13:1-7 and I Peter 2:12-17,
   and the laws of certain countries.

4. Exactness is demanded:

   * In interpreting the Scriptures.
   * In understanding the edicts.
   * In avoiding projecting our own personal traits.
   * In seeking a viable alternative to direct
     disobedience.

Issues and Insights

1. Strict interpretation of the Scriptures while re-
   specting differing opinions is called for.

2. In the growing tension between many governments and
   missions (and the churches), a greater awareness of
   historical precedents is needed.

3. Confrontation with governments is advocated by some.

4. A policy of submission to God, the God of history,
   would seem to indicate that seeking viable alternatives in our methodology while operating within the
   limitations imposed by the state is the best course.

5. Local authorities often interpret edicts in widely
   differing ways.

Special Problems
With Islamic Governments

Abram J. Wiebe

What I say obviously has a direct relationship to the
nature of Islamic government itself--its goals, its principles, and the type of society and mindset it produces.
This, however, is not my subject at the moment. Let me
also draw your attention to the fact that I have limited experience in the Islamic world, having been exposed only to
North Africa. This is, however, a heavily Muslim area; and
some of my comments, I believe, are certainly going to be
applicable to other Muslim states. I should like to divide
my remarks into three categories:

1. Problems relating to all foreigners.
2. Problems relating to missionaries primarily.
3. Problems between the Islamic government and the
   national Christian.

Problems Relating to All Foreigners or--Particularly as
They are Called in Muslim Countries--Europeans

It has been pointed out that for every American missionary abroad, there are a hundred other Americans engaged in
some other form of business or personal activity. It is to
these that I refer at the outset. These are the people who
obtain a job in their chosen country, come across for a
certain responsibility as outlined in a contract, and remain in that country for a significant time period. I am
not particularly referring to the tourist who has relative
freedom to come and go as long as he does not seek to reside
in a certain country.

Any such European who seeks to establish himself will be
subject to police surveillance from the moment that he
registers to the time that he leaves the country. Most of
the surveillance will not be perceived, but it will be
there nonetheless. Nothing will be said as long as a considerable distance is kept between the foreigner and the
national around about him. A certain amount of contact is
normal, but when this becomes very friendly, suspicion and
perhaps questioning could take place.

A second problem that the foreigner will come up with is
censorship of his mail. This has been experienced many
times in North Africa, and the general code is that all
should avoid anything that is political or highly religious
with regard to Islam. A certain colleague received a letter
from his father without the usual football scores enclosed.
Some time later, another letter arrived from a totally
unrelated person and the English football scores were enclosed in that letter. Another individual was asked by the
police, "We saw what they asked you, but we never saw the
answer that you gave." This censorship can be unsettling.

A third problem for all foreigners (and this is really
just one degree above the other two) is that of suspicion
because the foreigner represents a conflicting political or
economic ideology. I remember traveling on a train on one
occasion and discussing in Arabic various aspects of eco-
nomics. It wasn't too long after that I received a convoca-
tion from the police, and a rather grueling session of interrogation took place. The Islamic state fears for sub-
versive intervention and suspects that the foreigner and his
radio set or whatever other electronic equipment he may have
could well be the command post for such espionage or such
penetration into the country. A foreigner is always seen
as first of all a representative of his home state, almost
as an envoy. Therefore, all his actions are interpreted in
that light. When the foreigner--either by remarks, actions,
or just attitude--seems to make light of the existing political situation, his stay in the country very likely will
be shortened.

Problems as They Relate to Missionaries

(And I am thinking here in the traditional term of a
trans-cultural witness.) I would be so bold as to say that
50 to 75 percent of our problems in North Africa are related to the Islamic government. Not to say that there
aren't many other problems, but these are in the forefront.

These problems are of a political nature and are there because these governments fear a conflicting ideology which
could challenge their power or authority structure. In
most Islamic states, the status quo is maintained by the
strong arm of Caesar and the sword that he handles. It is,
of course, closely linked to their concept of the state,
which maintains that all power and authority come from
Allah; therefore, Islam rules, as it were, by divine right.
They further exploit the religion to maintain the unity of
the nation.

Inasmuch as Islam is the religion of the state, prose-
lytization is prohibited. In North Africa, this is further
underscored by the law which says that one cannot exploit
the other's weakness so as to advance his own convictions.
This is a punishable offense. One can change his beliefs,
as it were, by spontaneous effort, but not by inducement
from any other party. This is due again to the basic fear
that the governments have of a foreign, anti-nationalistic
minority group. I was told by a policeman in Algeria,
"We will not allow Christianity to gain a foothold in the
country again."

A second problem is that of residence restrictions. I
could include with that travel restrictions. A great deal
of time and effort is spent in getting the agreement of the
state to allow the foreigner or missionary to reside there.
His activities are carefully scrutinized; his economic
sources are questioned; and once approved, he is only given
a short limit, which can be revoked at any time. This
makes for a great deal of uncertainty and unsettledness. I
believe this is basically true in all Islamic states.
Travel is also limited. It is difficult to leave the country without going through the whole procedure of getting a
proper exit permit. In some places, it is virtually impossible to cross the border when conflict exists between the
two states, as is now the case between Algeria and Morocco.

A further problem is that of persistent explusions. One
never really knows how long that missionary will be allowed
to stay, and the past 10 to 15 years in North Africa have
been checkered by a continual strain of explusions usually
with very short notice. The puzzling thing to this is that
all too often no reason for the expulsion is given. Also,
at times this expulsion is preceded by months of questioning and harassment by the police, often to the extent of
great annoyance. In one case, the authorities broke into a
colleague's apartment to check out his files, obviously
thinking that he was some sort of spy.

Not only is the missionary's residence questioned, but his activities are also highly surveyed. When it comes to single strong action, such as publishing material, this is virtually impossible within the country. Most missionaries use small duplicators, but publishing a book is impossible, as is the free sale of Christian literature. Christians do not have the liberty to open stands in market places where they could sell or distribute literature, nor can literature be freely distributed in streets. Some bookstores which have existed prior to independence continue to operate, but these also are controlled and surveyed. In one case recently, when a piece of literature which was found belonging to a minority group, the bookstore was closed. However, since then, they have been given permission to reopen. Access to radio or television stations is forbidden to all foreigners--and certainly to missionaries as a means of spreading their propaganda.

Missionaries are commonly called in for interrogation, and one has to be ready for virtually anything. Usually a long series of routine questions is broken up by some very pertinent queries, such as, "Can you give me the names of the Christians in your town?" It is also stated by religious authorities that missionaries do not have the right to evangelize people who are minors. The head of the religious department in Algeria said that you cannot baptize anybody until you have taught for five years. This is even applicable to an adult. It can well be imagined that in most Islamic countries institutions in the form of schools and hospitals (as they are generally known) are not allowed. Gradually, with the coming of independence, these institutions have been taken over, as was the hospital in Tangier just a few years ago.

Other missionary efforts, such as the Salvation Army, have also seen their institutions closed down by the state. The basic reason given is that good works in this context are not allowed and that sufficient provision is being made from government organizations for the poor people's needs. Catholics, likewise, are progressively being forbidden to carry on their activities, in that their hostels and schools are either being closed down or taken over by the government departments.

Another problem, which I just mention in passing, is that of the changing of the day of worship from Sunday to Friday.

Problems National Christians Have With the Islamic State

Being what it is by nature, the Islamic government seeks
to control the cultural activity and thought patterns of
its people. This means that Koranic teaching is given to
all at an early age in all schools. This means that pre-
determined state ideals and programs are urged upon all
young people, and they are encouraged to become involved in
them. This means that state (and often Islamic) values are
held up as the very epitome of what the nation stands for.
All adults are encouraged to struggle for them. He who
would stand out against this tide is looked upon as either
a deserter or as very strange indeed.

The Islamic states allow for certain variety in their
minority groups, but they seek to dominate these and to
assure that Arabic becomes the basic vehicle of expression
and remains so. This is seen in the struggle in Algeria by
the Kabyles who are seeking to maintain a certain identity
over against stronger Arabic language sections. This opposition would even be stronger against a Christian minority. Christians often find that their movements are
controlled and surveyed, and it is not at all possible for
capable people or young men and women who want to train
abroad in Christian institutions to get permission to leave
easily.

There is a total identification between state and religion, and this simply means totalitarian government.
National Christians who do not completely identify with
this position are seen as turncoats and traitors to their
nation. This is especially true if they happen to be in
some sensitive position, i.e., a telephone operator who
might have access to certain material, or a soldier in the
army who might know something of the military capacity of
the state.

The most common result of all this is periodic questioning by the authorities and a careful screening of the believer concerning his reasons for affiliating with the
foreigner, or why he has chosen Christianity as a religion.
Not infrequently, rough treatment results, with threats of
more punishment should the individual persist in his views.

The fast of Ramadan is further used in many Islamic
states as a means of imposing on the total populace one
basic outlook. In some states, imprisonment can result
when it has been affirmed that the individual has broken

the fast. This is not merely the religious authorities ex-
ercising their power, but the government itself and the
judicial system.

Christian groups in Islamic states can usually be assured
that their particular cell of Christians is being integrated by Fifth Columnists, people who will listen and even
participate, but then later report the Christians to the
authorities. This creates a great deal of unease and is
directly contrary to any spirit of oneness and openness
that the missionary or national leader is seeking to
produce.

Islamic governments can be very harsh with decided
Christians--those who boldly and frankly proclaim their
faith. The most common pressure is that of harsh threats.
On other occasions, long questioning and brief periods of
imprisonment can happen. Physical mistreatment has also
come to pass. One brother came back from Lebanon where he
was attending a Christian school and was so highly inter-
rogated that he finally fled the land under his own impul-
sion and ended up as a refugee in France. It should also
be mentioned that Christians often find it difficult to
get jobs. Once their convictions and their faith are known,
the chances of employment are much reduced, especially if
the employment has anything to do with a government-related
position.

Summary

So, these are some of the basic problems with regard to
Islamic government. This is aside from pressure from religion itself, the family, or the individual's own internal
struggles.

We could say, then, that for the foreigner, his problems
would be in the area of surveillance and suspicion. For
the missionary, problems would mainly be in the area of
limitation and restriction. And for the national Christian,
his basic problem would be that of failure imposed by the
strong arm of the government. At the heart of all this is
the Islamic government's genuine ignorance of the Bible's
message and of the intent of Christians.

The government does realize, however, that the state
would never be the same were a Christian minority to establish itself in the land. It probably does boil down to a

contest for that power. Christianity is absolute in its
claims, yet tolerant and humanitarian in its expression.
Islam is totalitarian by nature and reportedly tolerant in
its expression; yet it is often violent in repression once
challenged. Truth can stand to be challenged. However,
falsehood of any kind cannot bear investigation or competi-
tion; thus, the bitter opposition from the Islamic state.

* * * *

GROUP FINDINGS REPORT

The Nature of Islamic Government

1. Totalitarian - Not politically but as a complete code,
   governing the totality of life.

2. Theocratic - Mohammed founded a religious state, not
   simply a state religion. Islam desires political expression. Muslim states today are struggling with
   the concept of an "Islamic State." Is it possible in
   a technological age?

3. Toleration - Islam is paternalistic to minorities.
   Ostensible to remain what you are or to become Muslim.
   But the law of apostasy has never been rescinded:
   "Whoever leaves Islam loses all rights and may be
   killed in service to God."

Possible Strategies

1. Care must be used by missions and missionaries in
   publicity and public relations in the homeland as
   well as on the field. Whatever is said or published
   in this country might come to the attention of a
   Muslim government and adversely affect opportunities
   for missionary work.

2. The opportunities for contact with government representatives and leaders from Muslim countries who are
   away from home should be pursued. Emphasis should be
   upon developing friendships upon an interpersonal
   basis. Lay Christians can and should be involved.

3. Many of the Muslim students in North America and
   other locations will return to become leaders in
   their countries. They are quite approachable and

appreciative of sincere friendship. Christians
should be encouraged and instructed in ministering
to these foreign students.

4. The witness of third world Christians residing in
   Muslim lands should be encouraged. They will often
   attract less attention from a Muslim government than
   will the Western missionary.

5. Political pressure by Christians in North America
   against repressive Muslim governments may ultimately
   prove counterproductive.

A Case Study: Korea

David J. Cho

When I visited the United States in 1956 for the first time, I was very surprised to see the national flag on the platforms in churches. In Korean churches, we don't do that. Our long-time custom, since the beginning of the church, is to allow only a Bible, the communion symbols, and the cross at the front of the church. So, to see a Christian flag on one side and the national flag on the other was very strange to me.

Also, the hymn books held a surprise for me. Either in the front or the back, I would find the national anthem. It was very different from our hymnals, since we Korean Christians are not accustomed to mixing a patriotic spirit and the Christian faith.

In Europe, I found that most of the churches had legal relationships with their governments, but in Korea there is no direct cooperative relationship between church and state. According to my understanding, this is also true in most of the younger churches of the third world.

Uniqueness of Korea Among Asian Countries

Korea is unique in its background. Most of the Asian countries were either occupied or dominated by Western nations in the past, while Korea was not. India was dominated by the British, Indonesia by the Dutch, the Philippines by the Spanish, Malaysia by the British, Indo-China by the French--and Japan attacked the West as an enemy. Korea

does not share this experience of Western domination. So
you don't find anti-West sentiment or "Yankee-go-home"
pickets in Korea. This gives a distinctive background to
modern Korea.

   Korea is unique in its self-identity. In Korea there is
one culture, one race, and one language. Most Asian countries are multi-cultural, multi-racial, and multi-lingual.
Korea will continue as a singular nation in this aspect of
its uniqueness.

   The nature of the Korean church is unique. The Christian
faith was introduced to Korea by Koreans; it was established by Koreans, and the Bible was translated by Koreans
from the beginning. The Western pioneer missions helped
the self-planted Christian process. Therefore, the nature
of the church was indigenous--an example before the term,
"indigenous," was introduced as a missiological term! This
is one of the main reasons for the strength of the Korean
church, for its fast growth, and for its ability to stand
on its own feet. Naturally, the growth of the church
brought Christian leadership to the nation--leadership involved morally, socially, economically, and politically in
the growth of the Korean nation.

   The resistance movement against the Japanese military
government, which had illegally occupied Korea, was mainly
led by Christians. Other social institutions were almost
non-existent. Until World War II, no distinction was made
between national and Christian leaders in Korea. This
background I have given to serve as a background to the more
recent phenomena of the conflict between a few church
leaders and the government of Korea.

Christian Influence Today in the Government of Korea

   According to the government statistics in 1977, there
were more than 20,000 Protestant churches in Korea and
nearly 6 million Protestant Christians--more than 18 percent
of the total population. The rate of church growth is more
than 10.3 percent annually--five times higher than the population growth. Most Christians are highly educated. More
than 30 percent of the higher government officials are
Christian. Since our independence in 1948, almost one-
third of the cabinet posts have been held by Christians.
As has been widely published, the total evangelism movement among the Korean military forces was led by high-
ranking Christian officers in the military. This all gives

evidence that no government can oppose the forces of Christ
in Korea. Although it is not a Christian nation, we can
say it is the most Christianized country in Asia.

In many ways, humanitarian service in communities, such
as rural development, health education, literacy work,
relief service, etc., has been initiated by the churches'
projects. The government has recognized these contribu-
tions as serving and developing the country.

I would like to mention several areas in which there are
various Christian activities which improve the cooperative
relationship between the church and the government.

1. Korea was the first Asian country which adopted the
   chaplaincy system in the military forces, and this
   program has been in use since 1951.

2. There are chaplains in every prison.

3. Chaplains are assigned even to non-Christian schools
   and are free to hold religious gatherings.

4. Ten years ago the police station began using chaplains officially recognized by the government.

In Korea there are various kinds of functional-group
movements which are unique and vital; for example, there is
one of the strongest Christian businessmen's organizations
in the world, formed 25 years ago. There are servicemen's
fellowships, taxi drivers' fellowships, an entertainers'
church, lawyers' fellowships, medical doctors' fellowships,
professors' fellowships, and numerous other groups. These
influence the functional groups of their communities.

Recently, however, some preconceived socio-political
Christian activities from outside Korea have been injected
through the ultra-liberal mission circles under the WCC.
For instance, Urban Industrial Mission was one of the
vehicles which caused a lot of hot issues.

My Personal Evaluation of Recent Issues of Church and
Government Conflict in Korea

First of all, the Korean church was ashamed of the misleading information which came through the secular news
media (and even some Christian media) which was exaggerated
and which overestimated the tension between churches and

the government. For example, a few years ago, an ordained
man was arrested and imprisoned. Some press release said
that "Rev. Park, a pastor of the First Presbyterian Church
in Seoul, was arrested and many church leaders are under
suspicion...." This news led the readers to look at the
Korean government as an anti-Christian one. The true story,
however, was different. The man who was arrested was a
part-time pastor, and his primary job was as Director of
Urban Industrial Mission. He was assigned to form People's
Organization in Korea under the guidance of Asia Commission
of People's Organization of Asia Council of Christian
Church, which is a regional body of WCC.

The name of the church was also misrepresented as the
oldest Presbyterian church in Seoul, but it was not--it
was one of the smallest ultra-liberal groups, which was com-
posed of less than a hundred. Most of the church leaders
don't even know where that church is located. Also, this
pastor was not arrested because of his faith but because
of his violent organization to protest the ruling government and to change the ruling power. He secretly planned
to mobilize the attendants of a sunrise service at Easter-
time to use them as a mass-protest force to oppose the
government. We have to think about the true background of
the misleading press release. I would rather give you a
chance to discuss this matter than to describe my personal
judgment about it. Often we see big smoke when the fire
was really quite small.

Do not try to equate the Orient with the rest of the
world. The church of Korea has a very strong selfhood.
Any kind of method or strategy of Christian activities
which may be relevant to one part of the world will not
automatically be accepted as relevant to Korean society.
The unnecessary tension between some church leaders and the
government came often because they tried to apply foreign
strategies. To make a long story short, let me point out
the following:

1. Why some missionaries were expelled.
2. Why some clergy were imprisoned.
3. Human rights issue and mass-protest.

First, the missionaries' expulsion. Korea is one of the
paradises for Western missionaries in the sense of the
freedom to proclaim the gospel. No rigid law exists against
Christianity, and there is unlimited liberty to do any kind
of mission activities--so much so that I wonder if there is

too much freedom! Not only is there freedom, but privileges are also given to missionaries because their work is not profit-oriented, but service-oriented. There is even no registration or permission required to start any new mission projects.

In the case of the expelled missionaries, their mission activities were not the cause, but rather their illegal activities of agitation to form labor unions and their mass-protest against the government.

Next, let's discuss the clergy who have been imprisoned. The reason for that was not because of their church activities but because of their politico-religious ties with minority opposition parties in politics. They were heavily involved in some anti-government protest, along with the anti-government leaders among the politicians. We feel very sorry to see this kind of activity. Sometimes these people use the names of the total churches to prove that the Korean church is a pressure group to the government of Korea. But this secular concern will not be agreed to by all the leaders of the churches at all. Let's distinguish between the divine goals and worldly objectives.

Finally, I have one more thing to say. It is about the human rights issue and mass-protest in Korea. Before we criticize the denial of certain rights by the government of Korea, we need to analyze the situation in Korea. We are in a war situation, even though we are a peace-loving people. We want to have complete freedom, but we have to realize we are confronting enemies. I have heard that during World War II people's liberties were limited in many ways for the sake of national security. During years of peace, we can have greater liberty. If we face an emergency, some activities of freer days will be harmful to us as a nation.

One day a young couple drove out in the country for a picnic. When they returned in the evening, they were admonished, "Don't you know this is war-time? Don't you listen to the government's requests to save energy? Don't drive for enjoyment but just drive for work." Everybody in the States had rights to enjoy driving, but it was not always so. I heard this story from a history professor; it happened in California during World War II.

We Koreans still can enjoy a drive in the country with our family whenever we want. But, for the security of the

country, some aspects of liberty are prohibited to protect
us from our enemies. A good example of this is that in
some international issues diplomats will not be allowed to
speak out if they are using the same line as our enemies'
diplomatic line. Mass-protests are also restricted. Sometimes any kind of mass-protest is taken by our enemies as
a sign of weakness, thus a victory for them.

So, we need to rethink these issues and give guidelines
to our church people as Christian ethics for social issues.
Using violent and non-violent activities to protest social-
structural evil is very sensational to the people in general. But we should clarify whether or not these means are
usable in Christian missions. These methods have been used
by Marxist international organizations in the past; now we
find them being exported to the free world and being adopted
by leftist Christian leaders under the name of peace and
human right.

Epilogue

The problem of evangelical missions in the third world
is naivete and indifference about these sensitive issues.
Most of the churches in Asia have some tie with Western
churches. So missions should be careful with any social
issues and political issues in their fields. We had a good
pattern in the past in Korea. The earlier missionaries kept
a well-balanced relationship between the church and state
and taught us when to cooperate and when not to cooperate
with the government. Our Korean churches grew under that
kind of godly guidelines, even in our relationship with
the government. On the other hand, we don't give the
government any power or authority over the church. That's
why we don't use national flags on our platforms or print
national anthems in our hymnbooks. The hymns should praise
God alone. Through this separation of church and state, we
can serve Christ in our churches and serve Christ in our
government duties--and express God's love in any place or
role in which we find ourselves.

* * * *

GROUP FINDINGS REPORT

Unlike the United States of America, Korea has no tradi-
tions of civil religion--no flag on church platforms, no
national anthem in the hymn books. God and Caesar are not

confused. However, it is the most "Christianized" of
Asian nations, with more than 18 percent of the total population and more than 30 percent of the higher government
officials calling themselves Christians. There are chaplains in the military, in every prison, even in the police
force; and there are Christian fellowships in every pro-
fession and function, from lawyers to taxicab drivers to
barbers. The gospel is everywhere present, if not in
control.

Since this is the case, and given Korea's long history
of nonviolent protest and passive resistance developed
during 40 years of "illegitimate" Japanese domination, the
question can well be asked: Why have some missionaries
been expelled, some clergy imprisoned, and the government
assumed an attitude of repression against mass-protest,
without full regard sometimes for human rights?

The answer given is simple:

1. No one has been arrested or expelled for doing the
   work of the church or mission. Repression has come
   for engaging in activities judged to be illegal or
   because of political-religious ties to minority opposition parties.

2. Korea is a peace-loving nation but is in a state of
   war; the capital is just a few jet seconds from the
   enemy. Perhaps the government should be forgiven for
   seeming to be a bit paranoid--and for postponing the
   exercise of complete civil liberty until after the
   aspired-for unification of North and South Korea.

The early missionaries and church leaders, living and
serving during the Japanese occupation, learned to keep the
balance between their duties to God and to Caesar. It was
a tricky tightrope to walk, but Korean Christians today are
still trying to maintain a truly biblical balance.

What recommendations could we make? National churches
need guidelines for Christian ethics in reaction to social
issues, and missionaries should be alert to distinguish between socio-political affairs and matters of proper social
concern.

Lessons to be Learned from the Church in the U.S.S.R.

Peter Deyneka, Jr.

The strivings and sufferings of hundreds of thousands of Christian brothers and sisters in the Soviet Union should stir us believers in the West--to compassion, to action, and to prayer. The church in the U.S.S.R. needs our help.

However, often overlooked and almost never publicized is the ministry of the church in Russia to us--believers in the West. The struggle of God's church to survive in the Soviet Union, a chapter of church history in many ways similar to the church in the book of Acts, stands as a source of spiritual strength, encouragement, and instruction to believers everywhere. And the church in the U.S.S.R., despite all opposition, is surviving and growing in Russia. (Currently, the percentage of the population attending church in the Soviet Union is higher than in Great Britain. Also, in the last five years there has been a religious renewal of such proportions among Russian youth that the Soviet government is alarmed.) What *is* the message of the Russian church *to us*?--to Christians in the West?

Stripped of most of what is considered essential in the Western church, *Russian Christians have learned to live and worship in simplicity*. Russian Protestant churches, which Soviet believers prefer to call *Molitvennye doma* (or house of prayer), are sometimes former Russian Orthodox church buildings--but more often former warehouses, log homes, or other simple structures; that is, if the Christians are fortunate enough to have a church building in which to worship at all.

The Soviet government usually permits only one Protestant church per city to register; that is, to meet with government approval in a recognized, registered building. The limited number of registered churches open in the Soviet Union cannot contain all the Christians who want to worship. Consequently, these Christians, and other believers who object to certain government restrictions on registered churches, often gather in unregistered homes and in the forest in the summer. They do not, however, consider themselves underground. They would say they are striving for open, legal recognition as is theoretically guaranteed them in the Soviet constitution.

Besides limiting the number of churches, Russia's atheistic government permits no Bible training schools or theological seminaries for evangelicals. Sunday schools are outlawed, and youth under 18 are not theoretically allowed to attend church or be baptized. However, young people do attend services anyhow and often are baptized.

Although atheistic literature pours from Soviet presses, it is impossible to buy a Bible or Christian book in any bookstore in the U.S.S.R., one of the world's most literate countries.

In desperation, some Russian Christians have begun printing Bibles on secret presses. Also, some Bibles are delivered to Eastern Europe from the West, although the amount is only a trickle considering the intense thirst for spiritual literature on the behalf of many millions in the Soviet Union. Believers behind the Iron Curtain are praying and fasting that their secret presses will not be seized by the authorities and that Bibles carried from the West will not be confiscated at the border.

Second, *the Russian church is a witnessing church*, even though Soviet believers lack so many materials which we in the West consider essential to evangelism. Christians are severely restricted from speaking about Christ outside their own homes, but theoretically they are allowed to teach their own children, and they do. Often, Russian Christian parents have large families because they consider the size of their family a way to expand the testimony of the church, which the Soviet government is trying so systematically to obliterate.

But even evangelism inside the family is not without hazard in the Soviet Union. In Soviet schools all children are indoctrinated in atheism from primary grades through university and are expected to join atheistic, communistic youth clubs such as the Young Pioneers. In the Communist clubs they are asked to write essays describing the Christian activities of their parents and are taught to inform on Christians. Some children have been removed from believing parents.

Despite all these hindrances, Russian Christians steadfastly witness, even to strangers. This is how evangelism is primarily carried on in the U.S.S.R.

Sometimes Christians ingeniously "arrange" witnessing situations. For example, one day two Christians, Anatolli and Pavel, were traveling by train. The coach was crowded. Anatolli turned to Pavel who was sitting across the aisle from him, "Pavel Ivanovich, you say you believe in some kind of a God. Tell me something about this God in whom you believe. How can you believe in a God you can't see?" Anatolli continued the conversation as though he were not a believer. Pavel thoroughly explained the gospel to his Christian friend while the other passengers in the compartment listened and joined the discussion.

Another witnessing Christian discovered a painting of John the Baptist with the inscription, "Behold the Lamb of God," in an art museum in the city where he lived. The Christian made a point of regularly visiting the museum. When visitors stopped to study the painting, he offered to explain the inscription. His witness was so effective that exasperated officials finally removed the painting from the museum.

As a way of witness, Russian Christians also search out opportunities to show kindness to nonbelievers. In a city in central Siberia an atheist agitator constantly harassed a group of Christians meeting in a home. When he did not come himself to disrupt the meetings, he sent *druzhinniki* (or civilian police) to disturb the worshippers. One winter the atheist agitator became seriously ill. Dying and desolate in the hospital, the agitator received no visits or comfort from his atheistic colleagues. The Christians, however, laden with food and flowers, came often to his bedside and told him of the living Savior.

Third, *the Russian church is a giving church*. One non-Christian woman asked her Christian neighbor, "Why are you *veruiushchie* (believers) always so poor?"

The Christian woman answered, "When we're poor, we need each other. If we don't share, we lose that blessing."

Fourth, *unity or oneness is another characteristic of the Russian church*. Although since 1961 there has been a division between the registered and unregistered churches in the U.S.S.R., Christians from both groups consider Christian unity vital. The separation of the *Initsiativniki* (or unregistered church) from the registered in the early 1960's came originally as a call for reformation of church-state relations, not just to form a new denomination based on peripheral doctrinal issues.

Constant opposition from Russia's atheistic government has been one factor in forging unity in the Russian church. Christians in the Soviet Union told me, "The authorities are constantly searching for a crack in our unity so they can divide our church. They try to bribe Christians to inform against other church members. In such circumstances Christians cannot afford not to have unity. (Before prayer meetings and communion, we examine our unity. If we have any quarrels with each other, we mend them before we pray or take communion.)"

Plagued for half a century by persecution and in some instances even prison and death, Russian Christians have had plenty of opportunity to experience unity and suffering.

Christians in Siberia, for example, told me about a meeting held in a house church in Siberia where the police came and started to pull people from the back of the meeting place out into the freezing February night. When the Christians at the front saw what was happening, they reached for their coats. "If you take one of us, we will all go," they told the police. As one body, the 150 Siberian Christians marched through the snowy streets singing hymns all the way to the police station.

Finally, *the church in Russia is a praying church*. One pastor in a church in the Ukraine told me, "In our country when we face persecution, we can't hold a protest demonstration. But we can pray--we can pray until the building shakes like it did in the book of Acts." He said, "We've seen more people come to Christ in our church recently than we've known for years."

All over Russia, Christians have designated every Friday as a day of prayer and fasting. On certain Fridays, the

believers pray for their children--other times for
Christians in prison. On some Fridays they pray specifically that God would protect the Christian radio broadcasts,
Bibles, and other literature being sent into their country
from the West at that moment.

On other Fridays they pray particularly for the church
in the West--for you and for me.

The story of the church in Russia's existing under pressure serves as a striking example to what the church should
be in all countries of the world and particularly for us in
the West with our opportunities and freedom. This is not
to say that the Russian Christians are spiritual supermen;
they are not. They are ordinary human beings who have experienced great grace for great burdens. Through their
trials they have much to teach us and can minister to us
by their example. Yet, we all belong to the same body.
We must not, in turn, forget to minister to them.

* * * *

GROUP FINDINGS REPORT

The relationship of the church in Russia with the church
in the West is a David-Jonathan kind of relationship of
mutual help and sacrifice. We have much to learn from the
church in Russia in terms of simplicity of worship, zeal in
witnessing, faithfulness in giving, unifying the body of
Christ, and depending on prayer.

In Russia the official religion is militant atheism,
determined to do away with religious thought. Atheistic
philosophy permeates the whole society. The Christian
faces a dilemma: being an enemy of atheism automatically
makes him an enemy of the state. In spite of this, there
is presently a spiritual awakening in Russia. Thousands
are coming to Christ. The Russian church is grateful for
encouragement from the church in the West.

During the discussion period, Stanislav Nasteka, a
leader, emphasized that those who might come under communism must be prepared to let their faith permeate all of
their being and to give up materialism.

PART III

Small Group
Discussions

Governments

A Christian head of state is assassinated; a Muslim leader takes over. The former government allowed religious liberty but was corrupt. The new government restricts religious liberty but tries to eliminate corruption.

PROBLEM

Are all governments God-ordained, or are some simply permitted? What criteria do we have for discerning what is ordained and what is permitted?

DISCUSSION SUMMARY

* Theological base is primary: Romans 13:1ff; Titus 3:1ff; I Peter 2:13ff; Christ's words, "Render to Caesar..."

* Criteria for discerning legitimacy:

   1. How was it established? (not greatly important).
   2. Length of control (only applies until control is recognized).
   3. Degree of control (whoever is in control *de facto* is ordained of God).
   4. Degree of acceptance within.
   5. Degree of acceptance without.

* Anarchy is not a legitimate government.

* All governments are placed by either the directive or permissive will of God; either is immaterial to us in terms of implications to Christian's lives.

* The ideal function of government:
    1. Restrain evil - I Peter 2:13.
    2. Maintain climate of peace (for proclamation) I Timothy 2:2.
    3. Praise the good - I Peter 2:14.

* The need of emphasizing the "warfare diversion" and the "suffering servant":
    1. American "comfortable evangelicalism" must be faced and dealt with.
    2. The "risk" element has been minimized.
    3. It was cautioned that the missionary's "speaking out" may result in damaging consequences to the national church.

* Practical:
    1. The degree of a Christian's responsibility to a government is in direct proportion to the legitimacy of the government.
    2. Christians are not to use violence to take the life of a ruler, even if his government is not legitimate.
    3. We are responsible to the government as long as we do not violate the higher decree of God.
    4. We cannot put so much weight on the word, "ordained," that we have no hope or means of instituting change.
    5. We can institute change through prayer, letters, and opinion polls.
    6. Government leaders are interested in public opinion and personal acceptance.

Ethics

CASE

Religious meetings are banned; believers hold meetings secretly.

PROBLEM

What are the ethics of civil disobedience vis-a-vis obedience to divine law? How far should Christians go in contravening civil law in order to maintain their faith and worship? How does this differ from situation ethics?

DISCUSSION SUMMARY

* What is the government's reason for banning the religious meeting?

    1. Is subversion being carried out under the cloak of religious liberty? In this case, temporary compliance may be advised.
    2. Is the government's stated purpose the true one?
    3. Has the government misunderstood the character and intent of the evangelical community? Temporary compliance while redress or appeal is negotiated may prove wiser in the long run.
    4. Are all public meetings banned, or just religious gatherings?

  5. Is the proscription against groups of any size, or
      large groups only? If the latter is the case,
      compliance without compromise is a valid
      alternative.

* What valid alternatives are open to the believing community in the face of a government edict prohibiting religious meetings?

  1. Development of one's own personal spiritual life
      (Philippians 2:12), though at the risk of a
      disregard of the duty of Hebrews 10:25.
  2. Dispersion - to rural areas where surveillance is
      not intense, or where the law is not in effect
      (Acts 8).
  3. Total compliance (Romans 13) - not desirable but
      may be a temporary alternative.
  4. Pursuit of legal redress through appeal or
      petition (Acts 16:37; 22:25).
  5. Corporate prayer (Acts 12).

* Having considered these factors, we may affirm that disobedience to civil authority (in terms of proscribed religious gatherings) is warranted if:

  1. The edict is contrary to the dictates of con-
      science in the light of the Word of God.
  2. If the intent is to eliminate Christianity.
  3. If the intent is to restrict growth of the
      Christian community (Acts 4:19, 20; 5:29).

* When contemplating civil disobedience, the believing community must weigh carefully the following factors:

  1. Have we gone as far as possible to comply with the
      laws of God within the existing law and system?
  2. Have we considered whether our disobedience will
      jeopardize others? Are we providing a scrip-
      tural model to the (unbelieving) community?

* Are we going farther than before? In other words, a
  government ban must not be allowed to occasion a more
  violent reaction (by the believing community) than is
  warranted. It must not provide a pretext for expression
  of wrong attitudes.

* Situation ethics differs from the above rationale for
  civil disobedience in that it is without moral absolutes.
  The Christian must view every situation within the

framework of God's moral law as disclosed in the
Scriptures, and he must then act in harmony with scriptural principles.

* What are the absolutes concerning assemblings, personal
copies of the Scriptures, etc., that are enjoined upon
man by God?

    The Christian may elect civil disobedience to
    secure a higher good, but he must be committed
    to endure the consequences.

* There is a danger of proof-texting, instead of recourse
to an integrated understanding of the whole counsel of
God.

* We have identified the need to do more serious biblical
research into the historical, cultural, and grammatical
aspects of the passages cited for support--or resistance—
to authority.

* The difficulty of arriving at an ethical solution to a
situation is inversely proportionate to our proximity to
the problem.

* We should recognize that we are pilgrims and strangers;
so we shouldn't be surprised when we are confronted with
two-world dilemmas, but we should be diligent to fulfill
an informed, biblical life style.

* No matter how diligent our preparation, Christ promises
His presence, power, and validation in the midst of
crisis (Matthew 10:16ff).

Politics (Nationals)

CASE

Political freedom and other human rights are denied to an ethnic group.

PROBLEM

What should be the attitude of Christian *citizens*? What action should they take? (Deal with *citizens*. Another question deals with the role of non-citizens, such as foreign missionaries.)

DISCUSSION SUMMARY

* In Burundi, 1972, missionaries endeavored to help the ethnic minority to escape, or to hide them. It was an overt activity. Some missionaries were expelled.

* Despite our American concepts, some nations are not capable of handling democracy as we know it.

* The missionary must weigh the value of the immediate against the long view in determining how he will address human rights issues, realizing that long-range teaching and influence might ultimately bring change.

* In Burundi, the missionaries were permitted to stay and regroup the shattered church, and subsequent revival came.

* The missionary must survey the whole picture and determine the course that will best enable him to fulfill his
  primary purpose of gospel preaching.

* The missionary can direct the prayer life at his church
  so that society is influenced by this intercession.

* In the light of the comment immediately preceding, we
  suggest that IFMA-EFMA could--and should--issue a call to
  our church constituency to set aside a designated day
  (set date) for fasting and prayer for the nation of
  Cambodia and similar tortured nations, praying for those
  in authority, that a peaceful and quiet life may be re-
  instituted in those nations. Also, we suggest that our
  Government should be notified of this action by resolu-
  tion and urged to exert all their influence to assist in
  getting U.N. action to halt genocidal wars wherever they
  exist.

Politics (Expatriate)

Political freedom and other human rights are denied to an ethnic group.

PROBLEM

What should be the attitude of Christian expatriates, such as foreign missionaries? What action should they take? (Deal with the role of expatriate missionaries. Another question deals with the role of *citizens* or nationals.)

DISCUSSION SUMMARY

* Under colonialism, missionaries had more opportunity and more effective protest. Present-day nationalism and independence make it more delicate today.

* Situations vary considerably, and each situation should be considered separately.

* Relationships should be built with the leadership of the national church, through Bible teaching, prayer, and example, before the issue comes to a crisis.

* Prayer should be seen as an instrument of change--corporate prayer of both mission and church.

* The missionary should maintain a low profile. As a
  guest, he has no right to direct appeal, but an inter-
  mediary or advocate among the national church should be
  found.

* Individual action should be taken to assist refugees,
  save lives, etc., where possible.

* Appeals should be made through letters to the editor,
  etc.

* We must be willing to lay our lives on the line in situations where God's laws are blatantly violated.

Rebel Causes

CASE A

A government expects and demands the loyalty of Christians, including church leaders and missionaries, and the active opposition to rebels who, Christians feel, have a valid case.

CASE B

A government expects missions and churches to aid its participation in rebel activity ("freedom fighters") in *another* land. Missionaries are asked to contribute to a fund to help the rebels.

PROBLEM

How should this call for identification with government or rebel causes be handled?

DISCUSSION SUMMARY

* The missionary must ever keep before him the purpose of his being in that country: as a herald of the gospel. This will guard him against getting involved in political issues that may threaten his confirmed, effective influence--or his remaining in the country at all.

* The missionary must have a long-term view and not endanger the continuation of the church's effectiveness long

after the dust dies down. He must always remember that
he is a foreigner and guest in that country. Political
situations are always ambiguous.

* The following principles should be adhered to:

    1. The missionary must declare the truth of the Word
        of God and allow the Holy Spirit to guide him
        and His people.
    2. The missionary must accept the work within the
        system to the best of his ability and take
        every opportunity available to carry out his
        ministry.
    3. The missionary must do good and show mercy to all
        men whenever the opportunity arises.
    4. The missionary's most effective involvement for
        change is his prayer involvement and his mobili-
        zation of other Christians to pray.
    5. The Christian must walk in the Spirit to be sensi-
        tive to situations and their ramifications, and
        he must be led of the Spirit in every response.

Socio-Economic Exploitation

The new elite have a monopoly on economic development and exploit the poor to the elite's advantage. The fat man grows fatter; the thin, thinner.

PROBLEM

What should be the evangelical attitude? Involvement? What practical steps can be taken consistent with the goals of the great commission?

DISCUSSION SUMMARY

* Possible involvements for evangelical missionary:
    1. Proclaim justice; let nationals decide how to implement it.
    2. Live a lifestyle consistent with proclamation of justice.
    3. Seek to do projects with the wealthy to benefit all of the community.

* Biblical teaching:
    1. A slave should serve his master as unto God, i.e., honest effort.
    2. A master should treat his slave as the Lord treats a servant, i.e., fair, considerate.

   3. In the church, persons are equal, despite economic
      and social status.
   4. "...turn the hearts of fathers to their children and
      the hearts of children to their fathers..."
      (Malachi 4:6).

* The new elite have a monopoly on economic development, and
  the poor are exploited to the advantage of the elite.

* New elite = Post-colonial.

* The missionary involvement:

   1. In Pakistan, establish friendly relationships with
      the elite to influence them (through friendly
      understanding and conversion).
   2. Conversion - one by one but within a clan.
   3. Training and education in a local environment.
   4. Help progress economically to independence.
   5. Teach biblical principles of living under oppression.
   6. Accompany the oppressed to court (with care as an
      individual, not as a "power structure").
   7. Long-term involvement.

* National evangelicals' involvement:

   1. Learn to live under oppression (Philemon, Paul's
      imprisonment) with genuine victory and joy.
   2. Biblical morality (hard work and honesty).
   3. Vocational trades to progress toward economic
      independence.

* Forms of exploitation--"Love of money is root of all evil."

   1. Kickbacks in letting contracts, etc., such as
      bribery.
   2. Wrong use of land - need for land reform.
   3. Patronage abuses.
   4. Inequitable taxation and collection, such as
      loopholes.
   5. Favoritism in the courts.
   6. Allocation of limited development funds that does
      not fit the real needs of the common people.
   7. Inequitable compensation systems.

* Possible evangelical options to actions and involvement.

* Disciplining a model community (light and salt) - this
  includes setting Christian standards. The Christian
  worker becomes the conscience.

* Develop a standard and practice that demonstrate these standards (such as adequate pay and work conditions, etc.) in agencies in which we have control.

* Using legal means of appeal to authorities on the part of the community.

* What solutions are there; what action alternatives?
    1. Change method of involvement - work as *insiders not outsiders* (involved innovators not just advocators).
    2. Broader concept of national leadership to be trained (for nation building, not just theological).
    3. Acceptance on an equal basis (no more paternalism).
    4. Development for their good rather than our good ("small" vs. "beautiful"; cottage church industry vs. multi-national industry).
    5. Develop responsibility ("this" vs. "ours").
    6. More lay involvement (every time this was used in history, it revolutionized the church).

SUMMARY

The ultimate answer is the changed life---but meanwhile, our first priority should be to provide functional models of the action alternatives listed above--and let everyone see them.

Caution! BEING COMES BEFORE DOING!!

Justice

CASE

Feudal landlords shoot peasants who refuse to pay exorbitant crop dues. The news is blacked out from the national press. The government knows that the only way the world press would learn of the incident is through missionaries in the area.

PROBLEM

What should/can the church and missions do in the face of blatant injustice?

DISCUSSION SUMMARY

* What is the obligation of the missionary? Consider the eternal value of the soul above the temporal.

* Possible actions:
    1. Appeal to central government office for agrarian reform.
    2. Shoot landlord in self-defense - defend property or family.
    3. Attempt to negotiate with landlord by peaceful means, through kindness and friendship.
    4. Consider relocation, especially in jungle areas.

* The missionary must risk himself, and he may be put out of the area, or his ministry will cease. This depends

somewhat on whether or not there is an evangelical church
there.   If so, will it continue if the missionary leaves?

* Is social injustice sin?   Is it sin to allow social injustice to continue without doing something about it?

* Sometimes we are acting as God, rather than as tools for
  God to use.

* What can we learn from early church history?   The early
  Christians witnessed and were willing to die for their
  faith.   Did they go out "on the limb" to interfere with
  social injustices?

* As Christians, we must be concerned about justice, but
  somehow we must find a proper balance and must find a way
  to continue our evangelistic outreach, while at the same
  time be concerned about injustices.

* In this situation, what would a *giving missionary* do?

Religious Liberty

Communication of the gospel in a certain country is banned. A missionary says we should go into the market and preach anyway - as the apostles did - even if it means imprisonment.

PROBLEM

What action should a missionary take in view of such a ban? What action should a national take?

DISCUSSION SUMMARY

* The missionary should not dictate to nationals what to do.

* The missionary should rely heavily on advice of church as to what he himself should do. But the missionary should be willing to speak up at his own risk if it would not hurt the church.

* It is valid to test the ban with a case to enable us to pursue the consitutional means of recourse.

* We need spiritual discernment to discover pre-persecution erosion of religious liberty so we can keep up the pressure where liberty may be threatened.

* Use nationals - Bible studies,
                  Word of mouth,
                  Nationals contact lawmakers.

* Missionaries:
    1. Conduct self as guest - respect law.
    2. Professional acting as lay missionaries.
    3. Recognize nationals to accomplish goal.
        a. Be patient.
        b. Walk correctly - be a model.
        c. Not cowardly but obediently.
        d. Knock on doors - test climate.
        e. Law interpretation.
        f. Proper attitude.
        g. Pray for situations.
        h. Be present whenever possible.
        i. Press for constitutional religious freedom.
        j. Disciple a cell group.

* Recognize that the whole concept of witness is involved:
  Life *and* lip, but in a variety of *forms*, including quiet
  ones.

* Think through what can be done - focus on the possible,
  and ...

* Don't panic; God *is* able; a fruit of the Spirit (but *not*
  our American culture) is *patience*: wait on God *and*...

* Look for the "cracks"; no system is airtight - there are
  usually options:
    1. Establish friendships - hospitality.
    2. Dialogue (*true* - two-way).
    3. Loewen's question method.
    4. Discern the social webs.
    5. Evangelism vs. mass evangelism.
    6. Teach Bible without Bible institute.

* Remember Revelation 12:11.

Benign Neglect

CASE

Some human rights activists charge that evangelicals show benign neglect regarding human rights and political involvement.

PROBLEM

How far is this true? How far justified? What is the reason? When involvement would endanger continued missionary ministry in the country, how does one weigh the priorities?

DISCUSSION SUMMARY

* Human rights and political involvement are closely related in most situations.

* Power of prayer - primary obligation in this political process.

* Enlighten inductively rather than through proclamation.

* Does a missionary by non-involvement create a wrong understanding on the part of the national Christians?

* The charge is unjustified. There is probably more involvement in human rights than the critics recognize. Such statements are usually unchallenged while no specific data is given to support such criticism.

* Missions' primary objective is church planting, *but* work
  in the following areas of human rights is always in the
  vanguard:

  1. literacy
  2. medical help
  3. emergency and disaster relief
  4. education

  It should be noted that approximately 70 percent of education in Africa is of church/mission origin.

* At the same time, we admit a weakness in reference to
  political involvements. We have taken a position of non-
  involvement, for we have felt that this is the proper
  position as strangers to the host country. We are re-
  solved, however, to take a more active role in certain
  areas. They are:

  1. Challenge the youth to involvement in local and
       national politics (three examples of success in
       this area were given).
  2. Influence and instruct the people in the biblical
       and righteous principles to be followed in
       government.
  3. Produce and have well-taught Christians of sound
       character in high places as soon as possible--not
       wait for a crisis to occur.
  4. Suggest that the Christian minority appeal to the
       U.N. charter when being limited or discriminated
       against by powerful religious groups.
  5. Intervene by way of correspondence to the foreign
       government relative to the legitimate concerns.

Issues

One tribe is dominating another tribe, exploiting it, denying it human rights. The mission works among both tribes.

PROBLEM

What issues do you feel evangelicals are neglecting? Why? What issues relevant to "Christ and Caesar" should missions be actively concerned with?

DISCUSSION SUMMARY

* Pray for peace.

* Supply help to exploited tribe.

* Mission may petition government.

* Missionary may give counsel to Christians about protest, passive and violent resistance.

Communism

CASE

Christians align themselves with a Marxist political party because this party is against a corrupt Capitalist government.

PROBLEM

How can we reconcile the cooperative attitude of Christians with Socialist governments which are openly atheistic? (Note: same applies to "religious" Muslims.) What different value system does this imply? What can missions do to help Christians understand the issues? What criteria do we have for distinguishing between crucial and non-crucial issues, vis-a-vis our scriptural priorities of the gospel?

DISCUSSION SUMMARY

* *Communism*: Example of Walter Gomez – Mexico – Former Catholic who was converted (lay pastor) and then later became a communistic supporter. Walter played the role of this man and stated the reasons for this. Grady Mangham played the role of a missionary attempting to answer the reasons.

    1. Reasons:
        a. Oppression of Roman Church
        b. Economic conditions
        c. Brighter future

2. Reasons for tension:
   a. Missionary seen as having political bias.
   b. National sensitivity.

3. Solution:
   Use other national leaders who understand
   Communism and can illustrate from their
   perspective.

* What is the value system of those in "third world" nations
  that make acceptance of Communism likely?

   1. Korea - North - Industrialized, nearness to Russia.
              South - Agriculture.
   2. Japan - Youth who are "thinkers" approach it as an
              ideology. As they mature and assume their
              roles in society, they do not follow
              Communism but become "liberal democrats."
   3. Africa - Nationalism - Communism rides on this.
   4. Vietnam - Also Nationalism - small percentage
                communistic.
   5. Western values - Individualistic - "Do it yourself."
   6. Many others:
      a. Community type of life.
      b. Controlled system - often from outside.
      c. Benevolent chieftainship.

* How do we help missionaries to understand the situation
  and, in turn, help the nationals (Christian citizens)?

   1. Be thoroughly acquainted with Communism as a system
      and understand the historical perspective.
   2. Close personal ties - communication - fellowship.
   3. Instruction - enlightenment - in institutions where
      possible without undue political implications -
      caution.
   4. Possible to approach under general umbrella of
      Atheism vs. Christianity.
   5. To understand their own ethno-centricism.
   6. Necessity of adaptability.
   7. Discernment - distinction between economic/
      ideological.

Preparing Missionaries

A missionary teacher examines a new math book prepared by a socialist government. She declares it is Communist and that she will go home before teaching from it. (The book does not teach Communism but is based on capitalist or free enterprise thinking.)

PROBLEM

How can the mission help their personnel to flex and adjust rather than snap or withdraw under adverse political climates?

DISCUSSION SUMMARY

* Every missionary must understand the political system of the country. If there comes a change, a takeover for which he was not prepared:

   1. The first rule is to not panic.
   2. A missionary must always remember that he is a guest and has no right to criticize the change.
   3. He must exercise extreme caution in counseling national Christians who come to him for advice or opinion.
   4. The Scriptures indicate that believers (God's people) can and should live godly lives under any form of government.

     5. Should there be protest, it must come from the
        nationals or national church, not from the mis-
        sionary or mission.

* We need to accept socially sensitive young people into
  our rising societies. After these young people come to
  understand the political, socio-cultural issues, they
  should then (not earlier) begin to witness in the host
  countries.

* The missionary must never become an activist in social
  change.

* The missionary must learn what/why a particular system
  is attractive/repulsive to the nationals.

* New workers must have a cultural-political orientation!

Participants

EARLE E. CAIRNS, Professor Emeritus of History at Wheaton College, is an ordained minister of the United Presbyterian Church, U.S.A. His teaching experience includes Western Bible College, Winnipeg, 1931-35, and Presbyterian Theological Seminary, Omaha, 1941-43. Dr. Cairns was professor of history at Wheaton College, 1943-77. He was Chairman of the History Department, 1948-73, and Chairman of the Social Science Division, 1969-75. In 1963, he received the Teacher of the Year Award. He gave the Lyman Stewart Lectures at Biola College in 1958, and the Legacy of America Lecture Series at Multnomah in 1976. In 1973, he was a visiting professor at Asian Theological Seminary in Manila. Dr. Cairns holds a B.A. from Municipal University of Omaha; B.Th., Presbyterian Theological Seminary, Omaha; M.A. and Ph.D., University of Nebraska. His writings include *Blueprint for Christian Higher Education* (1953); *Christianity Through the Centuries* (1954); *Christianity in the United States* (1960); *V.R. Edman: In the Presence of the King* (1972); *The Christian in Society* (1973); American Consulting Editor for Zondervan's *New International Dictionary of the Christian Church* (1974); *God and Man in Time* (1979).

* * * *

DAVID ADENEY is a former missionary with the China Inland Mission (Overseas Missionary Fellowship) and student worker with Inter-Varsity Christian Fellowship in both China and the U.S.A., and the International Fellowship of Evangelical Students in the Far East. He is presently Representative at Large for OMF, Associate Staff Worker for IVCF, and Vice President of IFES.

WALTER BAKER is Professor of Missions at Dallas Theological Seminary, and formerly a missionary to Haiti with Unevangelized Fields Mission.

DAVID CHO is General Secretary of Asia Missions Association; President of the East-West Center for Missions Research and Development, Seoul, Korea; and General Director of Korea International Mission.

W. ELWYN DAVIES is General Director, Bible Christian Union, and a former missionary to eastern Europe.

PETER DEYNEKA, JR. is General Director of Slavic Gospel Association.

R. MAX KERSHAW is Director of Research and Evaluation, International Students, Inc.

T. GRADY MANGHAM, JR. is Director of World Relief Refugee Services, and formerly a missionary in Vietnam with Christian and Missionary Alliance.

GEORGE W. PETERS is former Director of World Missions Research Center and Professor Emeritus of World Missions, Dallas Theological Seminary. He is presently Adjunct Professor of World Missions, Trinity Evangelical Divinity School, and International Consultant, U.S. Center for World Mission.

WARREN WEBSTER is the General Director of the Conservative Baptist Foreign Missions Society, and formerly a missionary to Pakistan with CBFMS.

HOWARD WHALEY is Associate Professor and Chairman of the Department of Missions, Moody Bible Institute.

ABRAM J. WIEBE is General Director of North Africa Mission.

Editors

EDWIN L. (JACK) FRIZEN, JR., has been Executive Director of
the Interdenominational Foreign Mission Association (IFMA)
since 1963. After serving in the U.S. Navy during World
War II, he returned to help found the Far Eastern Gospel
Crusade. Following four years as Home Secretary and
Treasurer, he served eight years in the Philippines. Mr.
Frizen is the recipient of the 1976 NAE Layman of the Year
Award. He holds a B.A. from Wheaton College, an M.A. from
Columbia Graduate School of Bible and Missions, an M.S.
from Florida State University, and is a candidate for a
Doctor of Missiology degree from Trinity Evangelical
Divinity School. Mr. Frizen is the author of numerous re-
ports, articles, and papers, and co-editor of the book,
Evangelical Missions Tomorrow (1977).

WADE T. COGGINS has served with the Evangelical Foreign
Missions Association (EFMA) since 1958, and as its Execu-
tive Director since 1975. He was a missionary in Colombia
with the Christian and Missionary Alliance for six years,
and has also served as a pastor in the U.S. He holds a
B.S. from Nyack College and an M.A. from the University of
Maryland. He has also received an honorary LL.D. from
Nyack College. Dr. Coggins is editor of Missionary News
Service; co-editor, *Protestant Missions in Latin America--
A Statistical Survey* (1961); co-editor, *Mobilizing for
Saturation Evangelism* (1970); co-editor *Evangelical
Missions Tomorrow* (1977); author, *So That's What Missions
is All About* (1975); and of numerous articles and papers.

Books by the
William Carey Library

GENERAL

American Missions in Bicentennial Perspective edited by R. Pierce Beaver, $8.95 paper, 448 pp.

The Birth of Missions in America by Charles L. Chaney, $7.95 paper, 352 pp.

Education of Missionaries' Children: The Neglected Dimension of World Mission by D. Bruce Lockerbie, $1.95 paper, 76 pp.

Evangelicals Face the Future edited by Donald E. Hoke, $6.95 paper, 184 pp.

The Holdeman People: The Church in Christ, Mennonite, 1859-1969 by Clarence Hiebert, $17.95 cloth, 688 pp.

Manual for Accepted Missionary Candidates by Marjorie A. Collins, $4.45 paper, 144 pp.

Manual for Missionaries on Furlough by Marjorie A. Collins, $4.45 paper, 160 pp.

The Ministry of Development in Evangelical Perspective edited by Robert L. Hancock, $4.95 paper, 128 pp.

On the Move with the Master: A Daily Devotional Guide on World Mission by Duain W. Vierow, $4.95 paper, 176 pp.

Social Action Vs. Evangelism: An Essay on the Contemporary Crisis by William J. Richardson, $1.95x paper, 64 pp.

The 25 Unbelievable Years: 1945-1969 by Ralph D. Winter, $2.95 paper, 128 pp.

STRATEGY OF MISSION

Church Growth and Christian Mission edited by Donald McGavran, $4.95x paper, 256 pp.

Church Growth and Group Conversion by Donald McGavran et al., $2.45 paper, 128 pp.

Committed Communities: Fresh Streams for World Missions by Charles J. Mellis, $3.95 paper, 160 pp.

The Conciliar-Evangelical Debate: The Crucial Documents, 1964-1976 edited by Donald McGavran, $8.95 paper, 400 pp.

Crucial Dimensions in World Evangelization edited by Arthur F. Glasser et al., $7.95x paper, 512 pp.

Evangelical Missions Tomorrow edited by Wade T. Coggins and Edwin L. Frizen, Jr., $5.95 paper, 208 pp.

Everything You Need to Know to Grow a Messianic Synagogue by Phillip E. Goble, $2.45 paper, 176 pp.

Here's How: Health Education by Extension by Ronald and Edith Seaton, $3.45 paper, 144 pp.

The Indigenous Church and the Missionary by Melvin L. Hodges, $2.95 paper, 108 pp.

Literacy, Bible Reading, and Church Growth Through the Ages by Morris G. Watkins, $4.95 paper, 240 pp.

A Manual for Church Growth Surveys by Ebbie C. Smith, $3.95 paper, 144 pp.

Mission: A Practical Approach to Church-Sponsored Mission Work
by Daniel C. Hardin, $4.95x paper, 264 pp.
Readings in Third World Missions edited by Marlin L. Nelson,
$6.95x paper, 304 pp.

AREA AND CASE STUDIES

*Christian Mission to Muslims - The Record: Anglican and Reformed
Approaches in India and the Near East, 1800-1938* by Lyle L.
Vander Werff, $8.95 paper, 384 pp.
The Church in Africa, 1977 edited by Charles R. Taber, $6.95
paper, 224 pp.
Church Growth in Burundi by Donald Hohensee, $4.95 paper,
160 pp.
Church Growth in Japan by Tetsunao Yamamori, $4.95 paper,
184 pp.
The Church in Africa, 1977 edited by Charles R. Taber, $6.95
paper, 224 pp.
Church Planting in Uganda: A Comparative Study by Gailyn Van
Rheenen, $4.95 paper, 192 pp.
Circle of Harmony: A Case Study in Popular Japanese Buddhism
by Kenneth J. Dale, $4.95 paper, 238 pp.
*The Deep-Sea Canoe: The Story of Third World Missionaries in
the South Pacific* by Alan R. Tippett, $3.45x paper, 144 pp.
Ethnic Realities and the Church: Lessons from India by Donald
A. McGavran, $8.95 paper, 272 pp.
*The Growth Crisis in the American Church: A Presbyterian Case
Study* by Foster H. Shannon, $4.95 paper, 176 pp.
The Growth of Japanese Churches in Brazil by John Mizuki,
$8.95 paper, 240 pp.
The How and Why of Third World Missions: An Asian Case Study
by Marlin L. Nelson, $6.95 paper, 256 pp.
*I Will Build My Church: Ten Case Studies of Church Growth in
Taiwan* edited by Allen J. Swanson, $4.95 paper, 177 pp.
Indonesian Revival: Why Two Million Came to Christ by Avery T.
Willis, Jr., $5.95 paper, 288 pp.
The Navajos are Coming to Jesus by Thomas Dolaghan and David
Scates, $4.95 paper, 192 pp.
*New Move Forward in Europe: Growth Patterns of German-Speak-
ing Baptists* by William L. Wagner, $8.95 paper, 368 pp.
People Movements in the Punjab by Frederick and Margaret Stock,
$8.95 paper, 388 pp.
Solomon Islands Christianity: A Study in Growth and Obstruction
by Alan R. Tippett, $5.95x paper, 432 pp.
Taiwan: Mainline Vs. Independent Church Growth by Allen J.
Swanson, $3.95 paper, 300 pp.
Tonga Christianity by Stanford Shewmaker, $3.45 paper, 164 pp.
*Toward Continuous Mission: Strategizing for the Evangelization
of Bolivia* by W. Douglas Smith, Jr., $4.95 paper, 208 pp.
Understanding Latin Americans by Eugene Nida, $3.94 paper,
176 pp.
An Urban Strategy for Africa by Timothy Monsma, $6.95 paper,
192 pp.
*Worldview and the Communication of the Gospel: A Nigerian Case
Study* by Marguerite G. Kraft, $7.95 paper, 240 pp.

APPLIED ANTHROPOLOGY

Becoming Bilingual: A Guide to Language Learning by Donald Larson and William Smalley, $5.95x paper, 426 pp.

Christopaganism or Indigenous Christianity? edited by Tetsunao Yamamori and Charles R. Taber, $5.95 paper, 242 pp.

The Church and Cultures: Applied Anthropology for the Religious Worker by Louis J. Luzbetak, $5.95x paper, 448 pp.

Culture and Human Values: Christian Intervention in Anthropological Perspective (writings of Jacob Loewen) edited by William A. Smalley, $5.95x paper, 466 pp.

Customs and Cultures: Anthropology for Christian Missions by Eugene A. Nida, $3.95 paper, 322 pp.

Manual of Articulatory Phonetics by William A. Smalley, $5.95x paper, 522 pp.

Message and Mission: The Communication of the Christian Faith by Eugene A. Nida, $3.95x paper, 254 pp.

Readings in Missionary Anthropology II edited by William A. Smalley, $9.95x paper, 912 pp.

Religion Across Cultures by Eugene A. Nida, $3.95x paper, 128 pp.

Tips on Taping: Language Recording in the Social Sciences by Wayne and Lonna Dickerson, $4.95x paper, 208 pp.

THEOLOGICAL EDUCATION BY EXTENSION

The Extension Movement in Theological Education: A Call to the Renewal of the Ministry by F. Ross Kinsler, $6.95 paper, 304 pp.

The World Directory of Theological Education by Extension by Wayne C. Weld, $5.95x paper, 416 pp., *1976 Supplement only*, $1.95x, 64 pp. booklet

Writing for Theological Education by Extension by Lois McKinney, $1.45x paper, 64 pp.

REFERENCE

An American Directory of Schools and Colleges Offering Missionary Courses edited by Glenn Schwartz, $5.95x paper, 266 pp.

Church Growth Bulletin, Second Consolidated Volume (Sept. 1969–July 1975) edited by Donald McGavran, $7.95x paper, 512 pp.

Evangelical Missions Quarterly, Vols. 7-9, $8.95 cloth, 830 pp.

Evangelical Missions Quarterly, Vols. 10-12, $15.95 cloth, 960 pp.

The Means of World Evangelization: Missiological Education at the Fuller School of World Mission edited by Alvin Martin, $9.95 paper, 544 pp.

Protestantism in Latin America: A Bibliographical Guide edited by John H. Sinclair, $8.95x paper, 448 pp.

Word Study Concordance and New Testament edited by Ralph and Roberta Winter, $29.95 cloth, 2-volume set.

The World Directory of Mission-Related Educational Institutions edited by Ted Ward and Raymond Buker,Sr.,$19.95x cloth,906 pp.

HOW TO ORDER

Send orders to William Carey Library, 1705 N. Sierra Bonita Avenue, Pasadena, California 91104 (USA). Please allow four to six weeks for delivery in the U.S.